PRAISE for *WTF to OMG*

"*WTF to OMG will teach you how to turn life's greatest curveballs into your best assets. Jennifer Sparks shows you the way with humor and empathy.*"

Cara Lockwood, *USA Today* bestselling author of *I Do (But I Don't)*

"*I wish I had this book 6 years ago when my WTF phase started! Jennifer nails it in WTF to OMG. She's your best girlfriend, life coach, and cheerleader all rolled into one. Tears and laughs and reality checks included.*"

Amber McCue, Speaker, Author, and Business Strategist at NiceOps

"*WTF to OMG is a hilariously inspiring guide for women who are ready to stop being a victim of their circumstances and start making their lives amazing. Jenny is candid, hysterically funny, and supportive. It feels like she is one of your best girlfriends, letting you in on her secrets and lovingly calling you out on your BS. I will be recommending this book to every woman I know!*"

Cara Alwill Leyba,
Author and Lifestyle Coach

"*Just by reading the name of the book you can be certain you are in for a ride! This book is for any woman who is breathing! In other words, it's for all of us! Even those of us who are already considered "enlightened" will learn something from this--this is a great tune up read for us practicing coaches! Jennifer's tone and her stories are completely relatable. There is no way anyone who reads this with the intent to change cannot become transformed.*"

Angelique Clark-Lawson, M.S., CCC-SLP, CPC
www.newleaf-lifecoaching.com

"*When you hit your WTF moment, Jennifer's combination of storytelling, voice of reason, and tangible action plans will have you swiftly working toward your own OMG life. Sprinkled with her personal experiences, Jennifer is easy to relate to and makes taking care of yourself as simple as 1, 2, 3. If you've been wondering how to get from WTF to OMG in your own life, look no further!*"

Shannon D. Caldwell, Transition Coach
Author, *Un-Hooked: Freedom After Divorce*

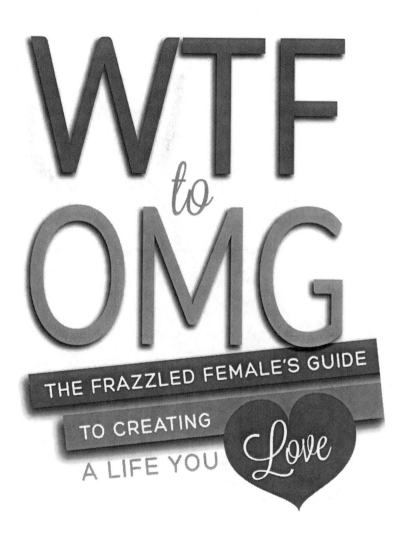

WTF to OMG

THE FRAZZLED FEMALE'S GUIDE TO CREATING A LIFE YOU *Love*

JENNIFER SPARKS

STOKE Publishing
www.swiftkickfitness.com

For my children, Frogger and Bean.
Thank you for teaching me valuable lessons every day and for all your love, laughter, encouragement, and support. This life would not be so gloriously OMG if you two pickle heads were not part of it. I love you both to the moon and back!

For my family.
What a journey we have had together. I am grateful beyond words.

Contents

Foreword

My name is Karen. I have had the opportunity to travel the world teaching and learning. I seek out opportunities for personal growth. I have an open mind and keep adding to my understanding of what defines an amazing life. I know Jennifer Sparks personally. In fact, I am mentioned in her book and was with her at the beginning of her journey. I have seen her transformation with my own eyes and I have been privy to her struggles and triumphs. She is the real deal. She is warm, approachable, flawed, and entertaining. We have been friends since the WTF days.

She asked me to read her book and give her some feedback. I was excited to see what she had created and to read her message. She did not disappoint. I made personal connections throughout the book and I know you will too. This book is for **every woman**.

Jennifer is a teacher and a storyteller. Weaving real life examples into this guide makes her message clear and practical. We see her stumble. We learn how she moves through difficult times and she provides us with strategies we can apply to our own lives right now to make them happier. Jennifer managed to stop at a moment in time when she felt that sense of overwhelm that so many of us are familiar with. She woke up to her own unhappiness and dissatisfaction, and took a step in a new direction. She found her inner voice and listened to it. She sought out the clarity to create action steps with a sense of purpose.

In turn, Jennifer leads us to awaken the little voice that dwells within all of us. The voice we often try to quiet as our personal needs become secondary to everything else around us. Capturing this process and nailing it down with her honest approach is her gift to all of us.

Her voice of reason and common sense is coupled with action steps for how to simplify AND enrich your life to make it more meaningful. *WTF to OMG* provides a solid structure for how you can live a life with purpose and courage while creating the mindset for the life you deserve.

This book is the story of her journey along with examples from others she has worked with or known. She genuinely wants to make a difference. Let this book be a step in a new direction for YOU. I urge you to open your mind and heart to allow her to assist you in the creation of your OMG life. I love *WTF to OMG!*

Karen Cooke (Cookie)

Introduction:
JUMPING INTO THE ABYSS

We all start somewhere. I was twenty-nine. I was unhappy. I had reached a point where I had made some mental promises to myself that by the time I was thirty I would have a radically different life. Well, change takes time. Change also happens faster if you have a plan and if you actually know where you are going. It wouldn't have taken me so long to organize my totally out-of-control life, if I'd had any idea what I wanted, where to start, or what to do.

I was stuck. I was exhausted. I was overwhelmed. I didn't really know how to define happiness for myself. I needed something different, but I couldn't clarify what different was. I thought I had made all the right choices. I had tried to do things the way it was "supposed" to be done: Education + Marriage + Good Choices + Children = Dream Life. I loved some aspects of my life but not how it was put together. I was agitated and confused. And I was really angry that I had allowed my life to turn out this way. Have you ever felt like that?

I was also really scared. My fear of doing something wrong kept me frozen and indecisive. I had so many parts of my life that needed fixing I felt like I was trying to eat an elephant whole. My relationships seemed void of emotional connection. There was no work-life balance, and I had a persistent sense of failure because my kids (who we had wanted so badly and conceived through emotionally draining infertility treatments) spent way too much time in day care while I tried to get my career established. I was forty pounds overweight and was out of breath bringing laundry up the stairs. My body was fueled on caffeine and sugar, and my crash landings were severe. I was beginning to suffer from chronic pain that doctors couldn't explain. I had very low self-esteem and worse yet, no self-compassion. I hated myself. I felt like I was standing at the base of a very steep mountain and I wasn't equipped to make the climb.

When I first made the conscious decision to change my life, I had no idea how hard of a road it would be, how long it would take, or what might happen. Uncertainty surrounded me like a dense fog. All I knew for sure was that I had boxed myself into a life with no hope. I had created rules and expectations that didn't allow me to breathe, and I had destined everyone in my life with the same fate. Quite simply, if I'd stayed in that life with those rules and with those expectations, I would have had no hope of anything better. And, neither would anyone else. I wanted better for all of us. **I was totally committed to change.**

So, how do you eat an elephant?
You eat an elephant by taking one bite at a time and you can change a life by taking the same approach. I took one step. It was a very small one. A miniscule shift: I started moving away from things that didn't make me feel good. **The mere ACTION of moving away from what made my guts twist and my heart ache began to move me towards things that made me feel better.** I started to sense a shift in energy. I started to see hope peeking at me from the smallest of cracks, letting me know it was still there, patiently waiting for me. This taught me to pay attention to my intuition. I stopped ignoring how things made me feel and started using my feelings as a way to navigate the unknown. Slowly, the fog lifted.

At the time, I was married, working with my husband to get a business off the ground, while teaching full time, and raising two kids under four. We were both working non-stop. My life was totally off kilter and out of balance. I ate a processed food diet and hardly slept. I was chronically sleep-deprived because my daughter woke up crying several times a night and was a horrendously poor sleeper. Until she had tubes put in her ears at four, she had never slept through the night (not even when the doctors tried tranquilizers). That was a very long four years.

I had no time to think ahead to prepare my days. I was in a full-throttle, reactive state. Day care had my babies and most of my paycheck. I couldn't organize myself enough to make choices so life was happening TO me. I was at the bottom of my own priority list. The students I taught got the best of me, and my own young children got the haggard, exhausted scraps. Being torn between being the mother I had always dreamed of being and building a professional career ate away at me constantly.

I had slowly given up all the things that brought me joy (friends, outdoor activities, hobbies, travel) for things that didn't mean anything to me at all (acquiring material possessions, ticking things off a list, living the dreams of others). I had also given up on myself. At times, I remember hearing myself say I didn't care about the life that was falling apart around me. I know I did care, I just didn't know how to communicate it in a way I could be heard. I also remember numbness, alienation, and a severe emotional disconnection to everything. I was unable to cry despite how much sadness I had crammed into my heart.

I didn't know it at the time, but figuring out how to be my best self was exactly where I needed to start and then all the other details would begin to fall into place. Believing in my heart that it was okay to work on figuring this out took a certain level of faith, especially since my life was falling apart around me. **But, healing is an inside job. No one can do this work for you. You truly have to start at the core. I realized this wasn't about my relationships with others or my job. It was about my relationship with myself.**

My lack of mindful decision-making in previous years, created the circumstances for a perfect storm. I had robbed my children and husband of the best version of me. I was doing all I could to simply stay afloat. There was no plan. It was time to put my big girl panties on and accept responsibility for my part in what my life had become. I had to be fully prepared to face the chaos that was going to transpire if I was ever going to move through this "place" to a new life.

It became clear to me that my only choice was to face my fear of the unknown, with a faith that I had not yet refined, and jump into the abyss. All the while hoping, praying, and believing that somehow I would land on my feet. I didn't exactly "stick" my landing. There was plenty of stumbling and arm flailing as I tried to keep my balance but eventually I discovered what worked.

This book shares what I have learned in this decade-long journey. It discusses how I moved from feeling miserable and overwhelmed to feeling grateful and alive. How did I change my mindset and take my life from WTF to OMG? Keep reading! I've speckled the chapters with stories from my own life and a mixed bag from personal training & lifestyle coaching clients as well. Some will make you laugh, others may make you cry, and some may really hit home. Each story will teach you something about the change that may be required to create a life you love.

After reading this book you will:

- Be considerably more **aware** about the choices you are making (or not making) and the impact on your happiness and quality of life.
- Understand how to **use your mindset** to change the direction of your life and get exactly what you want.
- Possess some **tools and strategies** for CHANGING your mindset so that you can start creating a life you love RIGHT NOW!
- Understand what to do when you slip and make mistakes so that you carry on and **find your personal sweet spot** for change!

My hope is that you will see some part of yourself in these lessons and stories, and if you are struggling, you will connect with something I say. I hope you will come to understand what thoughts you can tweak in your own mind so you can create a life you completely love. I hope to inspire, save you struggle and time, and give you some tools you can use to get out of a funk and move into a fabulous new mindset. If you find yourself standing at the base of a mountain preparing to make a climb like I was, I am offering you some strategies to make it much easier.

There is a free downloadable "WTF to OMG Journal" available at www.swiftkickfitness.com that has thinking space for you to record your ideas and responses to the SWIFTKICK TIPS mentioned throughout this book should you be inclined to record your journey. I highly recommend you have one place to record your thoughts. Also feel free to Tweet me your questions and comments at @SwiftKickFitnes with the hashtag #wtfomgbook to connect with me and other amazing women around the world reading this book, asking questions, realizing what has held them back, and supporting one another towards an OMG LIFE!

What are YOU going to do with your one and only life? This is completely up to you, so let's get started!

PART 1:
The BIG Problem - Your WTF Life

A true WTF Moment makes you aware of your current reality. It demands you accept full responsibility for where you are and it gives you the vision to commit to change.

In this first section of WTF to OMG, we are going to look specifically at the BIG problem: your current state of "WTFness." Big problems require big solutions so we will examine what a WTF Moment is and why it is such a powerful change agent. If you are sitting at the bottom of the barrel scraping the sides trying to figure a way out, find comfort in knowing that help is on its way!

We will also examine how a shift in mindset can change your entire life. Sure you have heard it all before, choose your attitude, blah, blah, blah, but I have some stories that will hit home and make the point stick on a level you can relate to emotionally. You will also figure out how to find out who you REALLY are and what you really want so you can be true to yourself. Sprinkled throughout the book you will find SWIFTKICK TIPS, actions you can take NOW that will start changing your mindset and your life. If you had nothing left, no one to judge you, no fear, and no baggage, who would you be?

The goal here is to strip you down and make you aware of the conditioning that has impacted your choices or lack thereof. At times, I am going to ask you to dig deep and be brutally honest with yourself. I am going to ask you to pay close attention to your feelings because that is where your intuition resides. We are going to access your ways of knowing and in doing so, we are going to rebuild you from the head down and the heart out. But, YOU have to be prepared to do the work.

Chapter 1:
YOUR WTF LIFE

Come sit with me and let's have a chat. I know you picked up this book because something about it caught your eye. You read the title and thought, "Hey that's me! I AM frazzled. I am feeling very WTF-ish. I DO want to create a life I love!"

While none of us share the same struggles, we all have them. So why don't you grab a drink and find a comfy place to sit while I share how I took control of my life and steered it away from WTF and towards OMG.

As a woman who has recently lurched past the forty-year mark, I would like to tell you that I did so with grace, authority, and a sense of control but that would be a complete lie. Most of my "living" up to this point had been speckled with triumphs, failures, tears, laughter, hard work (not always smart work), joy, disassociation, despair, anxiety, depression, anger, regret, fear and at some point ... white trash scrappiness. There were also some fairly long stints of struggle due to various "unexpected life events" or curve balls as I call them. The only common threads that have existed throughout my 40-something years are my sense of "ha ha" and my understanding that things could always be worse. Always. Looking back now I realize my journey thus far was about merely living life, not about feeling ALIVE. Until, that is, my WTF moment.

I was like a million other people out there meandering mindlessly through daily life when, one day, I woke up wondering WTF happened to my big dreams and my heart full of hope. Why was I so sad? WTF happened period? Where did my life go?

I looked at myself in the mirror and kept hearing that voice inside my head screaming, *"It's up to YOU to stop this madness! Slow down. Think things through. Get the hell off this sucker train. Find out what you want! Stop being afraid of the boogeyman and get your shit together, girlfriend! Surely, THIS is not what you are going to do with your one and only life!"*

That voice was scrappy. That voice wasn't going to just let me have it once. Oh no, that voice was dead set on waking me up and getting my ass in gear! That's the voice you hear when you hit the bottom of the barrel. It makes you feel like fighting. And that was the day everything began to change.

The WTF Moment

A WTF Moment (other aliases include Rock-Bottom, End of Your Rope, and Enough is Enough) is a pivotal realization that you can't keep doing what you are doing and expect things to get better or change. Sometimes it hits out of the blue when a "curve ball" kicks it off into the atmosphere (like an illness or a broken relationship). Other times, The WTF Moment builds slowly over time and then lets you have it with a fierce and unforgiving smack to the head. Either way, a WTF Moment becomes a very powerful agent of change. It becomes the moment when everything shifts and you begin heading off in a new direction.

A true WTF Moment makes you aware of your current reality. It demands you accept full responsibility for where you are and it gives you the vision to commit to change.

One thing about a true WTF Moment that differentiates itself from other moments of random clarity or awareness is that a true WTF Moment never allows you to pass the blame for your current state of affairs to anyone else. Yes, people may have done wrong by you but that can't matter anymore. No more victim mindsets. The WTF Moment eats that shit for breakfast.

It is abundantly clear in a WTF Moment that if anything is to change it will be up to you to change it. Your life is YOUR responsibility. If you are unhappy, YOU have to take control of changing it. If you are out of shape and miserable, guess whose job it is to make sure that you work out and eat right? If you hate your job, YOU get to decide what your alternatives are for employment. This realization, while simple and often evasive, is quite the little power pill.

The flip side of this newly claimed responsibility for your life is that when you accept one hundred percent responsibility for yourself, you must return the responsibility that you have taken on from others that, in all reality, belongs to them not to you. You are NOT responsible for the happiness of others, the kids' homework, your best friend's unraveling marriage, or the mood of the bus driver. Handing back the responsibility you have erroneously claimed as yours is critical so that you can create the time and space in your life that YOU NEED to focus on the one person you can control: YOU.

Have you ever heard the Polish Proverb, "Not my circus, not my monkeys?" It is time to focus on you and to encourage others in your life to focus on taking responsibility for their own lives.

When I had this "responsibility epiphany," I sat down with my kids and told them they would be in total control of their lives and their choices where it was prudent for them to have that role. With that responsibility of making their own decisions and choices based on their own wants and needs, was the understanding that they owned the consequences for their choices as well. If they wanted to be "big enough" to make the choices, they get to enjoy the consequences, too. You do not get one without the other. If they decide not do their homework until the night before it is due, their consequence may be that they are staying up late to finish alone because I will be going to bed and getting a restful sleep. If we start this "responsibility exposure training" early enough, we stop rescuing our kids, and we create more responsible children. And then, we have a little more space to b.r.e.a.t.h.e. Can you think of any responsibility you have erroneously claimed that you need to return to its rightful owner?

WTF Moments that appear to strike out of the blue, really don't. More often than not they are a result of series of events with the final event seeming almost trivial (like stubbing your toe or someone arriving late). However, that final event breaks your awareness open like a watermelon dropped from a second story window. There is no going back. You perceive the world differently. Your reality is forever changed.

And when the change starts, you may find yourself listening to an inside voice that begins chewing you out. This inside voice serves a very specific purpose. It is here to hand you your ass on a platter. It is NOT trying to be mean, it is being real. Mine went something like this:

"What the hell are YOU doing? You need some serious help. You are lost. You are bagged. You are fat and out of shape. You eat like crap. You sleep like crap. Your car looks like hell. Your fingernails are chewed to the bone. You fidget like a drug addict because your mind is on overdrive. You don't

do anything you enjoy anymore. Hell, you don't even know what you like anymore. You keep saying yes to more work responsibilities that you do not need. You feel disconnected. Your face has no emotion. None. Your eyes are dead. You hate your job. You don't care about anything. Your hair needs to be cut. Your skin is too dry. You are sad. Your eyebrows have grown together. You have totally given up. And, those pants you just bought are already too tight. You deserve more from yourself than this. Haven't you had enough yet? Gawd, get a grip!"

I was really angry with myself.

At times when I felt so deflated and exhausted, that voice was a little kinder but it always had the same message,

"Come on, you know you deserve more than this. You know you are not happy. You know this doesn't feel good anymore. You know only you can change it. Enough is enough. It's time to DO something about it."

Unlike the other voices that tell you things based entirely on limiting belief systems which are aimed to deflate you, render you feeble, and keep you stuck (you are a loser, you are lazy, you will never amount to anything), the WTF voice arrives with the sole purpose of giving you a big slap to the head to wake you up and to get you moving in the direction of purpose, clarity, and bliss. Sometimes, it is a little rough.

The WTF voice just tells you what it sees. If the timing is right and you are open to the message, the sudden awareness catapults you into a new way of thinking about yourself and your life. It begins with you taking stock of how you really, truly, honestly feel about where you currently are in life.

Chapter 2:
CONTEMPLATION BEGINS

Once my WTF Moment had spoken I began contemplating the truth in its words.

"I do drag my sorry, exhausted, passionless ass out of bed every single day. Each day at the same time I do the same things. I eat the same crappy food and when someone asks me how I am, I answer with the same lie. 'Oh, I'm good and how are you?'

I have shut my mind off and I just do what needs to be done. I do not make a single choice with any sense of intention. The sun comes up, the sun goes down and what exists in between just gets done. I never question. I understand that the sooner it is all done, the sooner I can collapse, totally wrecked, into my bed like a wounded water buffalo. There is no prize earned here for finishing. I 'enjoy' a restless and unfulfilling sleep and start all over again in the morning.

I am so busy and sleep deprived that I have not even had the time to actually realize how stupid it is that I am this busy, this burned out, this disconnected, and this unaware. I am walking a fine line between a full-blown breakdown and a critical uprising. I do not even know how precariously I am walking this line. If I was to be honest with myself, my mood one day (which is based on uneducated food choices, poor sleep patterns, and a negative outlook) may be the only thing that determines if I am going over the wall to something better or into a mental ward. It's a fine, fine line."

I come to understand THIS voice is trying to save me. This was my truth, my reality. I was ready for change.

Likely you have had one, two or maybe even several moments when you were struggling with life and craving something more. Sometimes we have them and roll right back over and ignore them. Too tired. Timing isn't right. It's all too much. There is a difference between knowing what needs to be done and doing it. But sometimes we just have to do it regardless of how impossible it seems at first glance.

I remember vividly the day I decided I was D.O.N.E. Done being exhausted. Done being fat and out of shape. Done suffering from unexplainable chronic pain in my arms and neck. Done serving the needs of everyone, except myself. Done with having NO reserve tank. Done being sad. Done feeling hopeless. D.O.N.E. I was going to create time to think. Breathe. I was going to get fit. I was going to spend some time putting something into my personal energy bank. I knew I needed all these things but I didn't know exactly how to get it.

I had this brilliant little idea that I would train for and run a marathon (remember at this point I am fat and out of shape). First off, I had never been a runner. Secondly, I couldn't get up a flight of stairs without having my heart nearly explode. Thirdly, neither limitation mattered to me because I was going to pick something big and just do it. I was going to make a concentrated effort in ONE area. In fact, I decide I was going to help others (fundraising for Arthritis) while I did it and I was going to run my marathon in Hawaii as a member of The Joints in

Motion Training Team. I knew I needed help and this would provide me some coaching and support. I was going to get a vacation from my life, travel (which I loved), and fundraise for a great cause (in honor of my Dad). I thought this was an awesome plan. The only thing was I had to "learn to run 42.2 km."

I wondered how far I could run in my current state of ruin. One day after work, still in my totally unflattering mother-teaching slacks and teacher shoes, I parked my old man car near my local corner store, took off my sweater that hid my fat, and I took off running. I have since termed this "run" my rage run. I was angry with myself for letting my life come to this place of neglect. Exercise rattles your emotions. So as I ran, I had to run through some surprising emotions that were laying just beneath the surface, angered by the physical pain running was putting me in, the lurking emotions woke like a beast. I ran for what seemed forever. I was hot as hell. Sweating. Panting. Purple. Frustrated. Angry.

Forever turned out to be about three kilometers. But something unexplainable happened on that run. I sucked so incredibly badly that I couldn't believe this is what had come of me! But, I wanted to come back the next day and do it again. (With proper clothing, shoes and purpose).

Upon waking the next day, I went to throw my legs out of bed only to discover I could barely move. I was crippled and in excruciating pain from that little three kilometer run. The following day, the stiffness was even worse. I was stiff from where my fat jiggled. The meat between my ribs hurt. Every part of my body was stiff, even my face was stiff from grimacing. That just pissed me off more because this was not who I wanted to be!

I signed up for The Joints in Motion Training Team that would be participating in the Honolulu Marathon in December. A perfect hot holiday getaway in the middle of the Canadian winter! My crazy friend Cookie joined too! We had twenty weeks to go from no fitness to a full marathon and raise five thousand dollars each for arthritis.

I don't know about Cookie, but I bit off way too much to chew! Regardless, I was committed. I locked myself into it because quitting was not an option. I was so angry that I had allowed myself to turn into someone I didn't recognize. I felt like I wanted to punish myself. Running hurt. It was a perfect solution. I also had the group support and the fundraising accountability. I would do this, even if it killed me! (And even though Cookie moved to the USA shortly after, we raised our funds and met in Hawaii for a great vacation and a "run." I made new friends who I still keep in touch with over ten years later. Cookie and I still laugh about the post run adventures, which could almost be another book.)

I had learned a very valuable lesson looking back on who I had allowed myself to become. You cannot get a refund on time wasted. Finally understanding this on a new level changed the entire way I live my life.

You only have one life. ONE. 1. UNO.

You can't trade it in, nor can you extend it. And death, can visit you anywhere, anytime. You are likely NOT going to be expecting it. Death isn't usually something we have planned, which is ironic because it is one of the ONLY things that is guaranteed.

A WTF Moment is the beginning of a new life for you. It is at THIS point you know in the deepest parts of your heart that things really need to change. You want to change. You are prepared to do what needs to be done to change, even though you may have absolutely no idea how to begin. You KNOW it is time.

You start the journey by becoming totally aware of your reality. You begin making conscious choices that will move you into a new space. You begin to change your mindset, perspective, and understanding of what it means to live "your life" the way you want to live it. You begin to live with a new set of rules that YOU create with intention and care. Initially, these rules may not be spoken into anything formal, but over time as you grow, the new mindset takes hold and it begins to frame your life in a way that you become armed with a new sense of purpose, resilience, and control.

A WTF moment is really a SWIFTKICK in the ass that encourages you to claim control over how you will live your life. It empowers you. It energizes you. It teaches you the difference between living and feeling alive. It helps get you fired up to face the crap you might have to deal with to get to the other side of the swamp and up and over the mountain ahead. It pokes at you like a playground bully, until you finally "snap" and strike back with all your being!

The late Steve Jobs captured the essence of what I am saying perfectly:

"Your time is limited, so don't waste it living someone else's life. Don't be trapped by dogma - which is living with the results of other people's thinking. Don't let the noise of other's opinions drown out your own inner voice. And most importantly, have the courage to follow your heart and intuition. They somehow already know what you truly want to become. Everything else is secondary."

A special gift of The WTF Moment is that is gives you a fiery new sense of "who the hell cares" and you are less influenced by the judgment of others. This is a mindset everyone needs to possess if they are standing at the base of a mountain they need to climb because getting up the mountain is going to require a shitload of creativity on your part. You are going to have to go outside your comfort zone to overcome what holds you back. I guarantee it.

The WTF Moment allows you to loosen the shackles of outside expectations just enough to begin exploring new and exciting possibilities. As Ritu Ghatourey said, some "people wait all week for Friday, all year for summer, and their lifetime for happiness." Don't be one of those people. Stop waiting and start doing! And, NEVER let the judgment of others determine what actions you take to make your own dreams come true. The WTF Moment is a true blessing even if you are face down in the sludge, because change is brewing. It's YOUR time. One life, remember?

Why Life Balance is Just an Act

Life is forever moving along. Time never stops. If you stop, life keeps going on around you. If you decide to stay in bed for an entire weekend, when you wake up you will learn of things that have changed. Even though you had no active part in these changes, they still could impact your own personal life balance. It is a juggling act. My personal belief is that no one is ever truly balanced but that striving for balance is key to feeling good.

Is it possible to feed triplets at once? Nope, you are always a boob short. But for a few minutes, you might have all three babies satisfied enough to believe you are in a state of balance. Just give it a few minutes and then things start to shift again. That's just life. It is always moving.

True balance doesn't exist long term. One life element might have to give way to another at times, but I do believe the idea of balance IS something to strive for regardless of never being able to truly achieve it. Doing so keeps you from becoming severely crippled from a life that is indeed out of whack.

Consciously working towards balance forces us to pay attention to all the parts of our lives that bring us happiness. Grossly ignoring one part of our life long term for success in another part will not lead to happiness. We have all heard of the person who is successful and rich but sad because he/she is alone. Or, the workaholic who loses a relationship because their partner moves on to meet their own needs instead of relying on another for this sense of fulfillment. What about the young mother that dotes entirely on her children and forgets to care for her own well-being? Time passes and one day she wakes up in a bad place because her wellness has been sacrificed for years. Striving for balance keeps us from getting to these places of absolute desperation, even if we never actually achieve true balance.

It keeps you trying to be the best you can be. Maybe you have a few bad days of eating because of a deadline at work (so food preparation gives way to deadline requirements) but you meet the deadline. A consequence of not eating well while you were under pressure is that now you feel like crap. Now that the deadline has passed, you pull up your socks and begin taking care to eat well again. You immediately feel better and remind yourself that good eating habits are key to feeling good and being sharp in more stressful times. This is the ebb and flow of life.

Learning to be the best you can be means you examine situations where you stumble and ask yourself, "What can I learn from this?" As in the above example, the answer might be, "Next time, when I see a deadline approaching, I am going to pre-cook a bunch of meals, or get a personal chef to make some meals for my freezer so that when I am really under the gun, I can grab the healthy meals I have prepared and power through the deadline fully optimized with good food."

The key here is not giving up on one area because you stumbled. Many people fall victim to an "all or nothing mindset" and just throw in the towel completely. "Oh, I ate crappy for that week so I may as well just give up because I can't do it. I don't have the will-power. I wasn't perfect. I failed. I always fail." Some people feel if they can't do it right all of the time, then why bother. If you woke to find you had a flat tire on your car, would you slash the other three? No, likely not! So when you stumble, fix the issue but don't make things harder for yourself by quitting!

I urge you to be human, be patient when you mess up, forgive yourself, and do a great job as often as you can. Trust me, doing well eighty percent of the time kicks the pants off of sucking one hundred percent of the time. Remember, you eat an elephant one bite at a time, not all at once! Being your best is a matter of tweaking things until you find YOUR own individual sweet spot. Strive for balance but don't obsess over it.

SWIFTKICK TIP: Reality Check

Since the green tea (or the wine) has now warmed you up, let's just get to the good stuff. Let's just get real. How happy are you? Look at the life elements in the table (feel free to add any I omitted) and rate how happy/satisfied you feel about that area of your life. No editing! I am not going to judge you if you rate an area really low (in fact, if you do, you just identified an area to focus on), so don't go adding a few points in case someone picks up the book and sees how you scored things. Maybe they need to see it anyway. Move away from fearing the judgment of others. You have a right to feel exactly as you do but you also have an obligation to yourself to realize moving forward into bliss is totally doable, and entirely up to you alone. Stop hiding.

This is about you being honest and real. No more pretending. Starting now, you are going to strive to be authentically YOU. You are not going to worry about what Ma or Pa or Life Partner thinks about who you are and what you want. Yes, it's time to get real, baby, one hundred percent real.

Be open. Listen to your gut reaction. Read each word below and then score how you feel about that part of your life. If you give yourself a zero, that means you feel super crappy about it. If you are sitting middle of the road, perhaps you hear "meh" inside your head. If you do, that is about a five. A seven would mean pretty good, and a ten score means that part of your life is rocking awesome. You can use the scale 0-10 and any number on it. If a part of your life somehow is missed in the list below, add it in to better reflect your own life circumstances.

Got it? Good. Go!

Life Element	Rate (1-10)
Relationships	
Family	
Finances	
Professional/Career	
Physical Fitness	
Nutrition	
Emotional Wellness	
Mental Wellness	
Self Care	
Spirituality/Religion	
General Lifestyle Habits/Other	

Now imagine your life is like a wheel, with spokes dividing the many parts of the wheel into sections, and each section represents a part of your life. If a zero score is located in the middle of the wheel, and scores of ten are out along the edge, how balanced is your life wheel? Use the blank wheel below to create a visual representation of your life's snap shot at this moment. Pick your top eight life elements (or customize to include things I may have omitted). Make a note about what you see. What areas need the most work? What area's successes might rob from the balance of other life areas? What areas score low and what factors contribute to that low score?

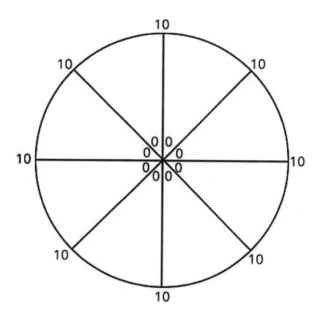

Don't fret if your wheel was bumpy and lopped sided. This activity serves as a way to make you aware of your life as a whole and to make you more aware of the reality of your life in this moment. Even people with super awesome lives are likely to find their wheel isn't one that always gives them a smooth ride. Life throws you curve balls and surprises and your reaction to these things can throw the wheel out of balance. Your goal here is to have a strong mindset established to help you deal with life's curve balls in a way that keeps you on a more even keel. Let's face it, life doesn't always go as planned so you need to have the mindsets in place to deflect a little bit of the impact!

PART 2:
The Big Solution – Mindset Shift

How we rise from the ashes, determines where we get to go from here. If you become aware of how your mindset can change everything, you can learn to view your life and how you experience things in a new way. Being knocked down can be a blessing.

Chapter 3:
SUCCESS BEGINS IN OUR MINDS

When you hit rock bottom the view changes. Imagine it like this: You are walking around doing what you do - day in and day out. You are in a state of "meh" or perhaps your life truly sucks by all accounts because you are not doing anything you want to do, you feel no passion, and you have no idea what it is you want from this thing called life. Regardless, you are still moving upright through your life. Then suddenly, life whips in a groovy little curve ball and you are knocked completely off your feet. A relationship changes, a diagnosis leaves you reeling, a job disappears and suddenly what you always assumed was certain and stable is no longer.

You come to and find yourself on your back, panting to catch your breath and recover from the blow. You open your eyes and the view has changed. You are now staring straight up into the sky. No distraction, just blue sky. Everything you previously knew is gone.

What a great opportunity to pick yourself up, dust yourself and show some grit. I know, you totally hate me for saying that but please hear me out. There is a lesson to be learned from what has just exploded forcefully into your life and it is your job to figure it out. Perhaps, there is something better waiting for you out there to discover and you needed to be in a place to be open to it. Is it possible that life is presenting an opportunity for you to learn how to be open in the way you need to be?

When bad things happen in our lives (or even without "bad things" happening), our perspective can change for the good or the bad. If you are aware about what's going on, you have the power to pick your perspective. You are in control of where you focus your energy. And picking your point of focus changes the game.

How we rise from the ashes, determines where we get to go from here. If you become aware of how your mindset can change everything, you can learn to view your life and how you experience things in a new way. Being knocked down can be a blessing. Divorce can be a blessing. Illness can be a blessing. Loss can be a blessing because of the lessons these types of events can teach you. (Please don't confuse this with not truly experiencing pain while you move though some of the things you need to move through). Ex-spouses can learn to be the best of friends. Illnesses can teach us things that make our lives richer. Loss, can teach us what means the most to us.

Imagine for a moment that your life as you know it crumbles and you are left trying to put the pieces back together. Yes, give yourself permission to be reflective, to grieve, and to feel the emotions of the event as you pull from it the lesson it holds for you. Speaking from my own experience, some of my darkest moments, hardest struggles, deepest pain, and ultimate failures have been my greatest teachers. I am now at a place where I can look back on these darker times and feel grateful for the gifts they brought into my life. I wouldn't change a thing. When I was stuck in them, I had to use focus to get through them as best I could while extracting what it was I needed to learn. I am a different (and I would argue better) person because I was able to learn something from each struggle and these lessons have allowed me to make positive changes.

I am not suggesting for a moment that you skip off into a meadow of wild flowers pretending everything is fine. Getting to OMG is a process, not an event. It is like having a blank canvas in front of you with no idea what you are trying to create. The external "rules" by which you previously lived your life can fall away when "bad" things happen. With that, you may be delighted to discover that many things that previously blocked your progress were released and you can now choose to explore and discover the bliss that already exists within you.

How you internalize what happens in your life can transform into belief systems that can help you flourish. Likewise, you can create a belief system that holds you prisoner and keeps you stuck. You must ask yourself what have you conditioned yourself to believe about yourself and about life as a result of the experiences you have had? Did your divorce leave you believing you were worthless? Did your inability to lose weight for your reunion convince you that you were, and always would be, a failure? Has your inability to conceive children made you feel like you are not enough? Does your daughter's drug addiction mean you are a horrible parent?

If you find that your belief systems and patterns of thinking cause you to behave in certain ways that hold you back, you must address your belief systems head on. You must challenge your beliefs and stay connected to the impact they have on your life and choices. Change the faulty beliefs and feed the empowering ones so that your refined belief system propels you forward into all that is great! Your belief system and perspective have an incredibly powerful impact on your default behaviors. The good news is you can change both.

If a change in perspective is required, as soon as you make it, transformation begins. The best news yet is that a small shift can yield dramatic results. A little shift at the core of who you are, maintained over time, can take you on an entirely different journey and to an entirely different destination.

Understanding that your experience and perceptions of an event can be completely different than someone else's is also critical because people may try to change your perceptions if they are not in line with their own. You don't need to agree, even if you both stood in the same room as something took place. Own your perceptions, because it is your responsibility to create your own reality. If you take from an experience a lesson that allows you growth and someone else takes from that same event a perception that drags them down and keeps them stuck, that is their choice but it doesn't need to be yours.

Another thing worth thinking about is that it is truly impossible to serve two ideas that move you in opposite directions. It is YOUR choice to decide which perspective you will feed. Pity parties, woe is me, and victim mindsets will get you nowhere. Understanding that perception is a choice, and not a fact, is key to understanding the power a perception shift can have over your life. I know that's a pretty amazing concept, isn't it? Your potential is limitless.

Perception Creates Your Reality

How many times have you heard someone say, "Now that I am out of the relationship, I see things so much more clearly?" Being submersed in the problem can blind us from seeing the solutions. My Dad used to always say; "It is hard to see the forest when your face is against the bark of a tree!" It can cripple our creativity and problem solving abilities. It can render us useless and that is when we can really get stuck. But, all you have to do is step away from the situation long enough to clear your head. Begin exploring the many alternative perspectives you could have of a given event, in addition to the one you currently hold. How you choose to perceive things is up to you, and your perspective can be a truly magical way to dance through really hard times. Trust me.

Let's Talk About Curve Balls & Lessons

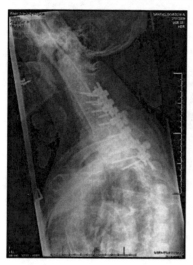 My first Ironman triathlon race was to be in August of 2008 in Penticton, British Columbia. I had trained for a year to transform my fitness levels to a point where I would be able to swim the 3.8 kilometer open water swim, cycle 180 kilometers through the mountains, and then run the 42.2 kilometer marathon at the end. I was three weeks out from the race and feeling pretty good with how things were coming together. I was just getting ready to begin my taper to give my body a chance to rest and recover so it could be prepared for race day. I had a light run to do on this particular day and was headed out just as my cell phone rang.

"Hi, it's Mom. What are you up to?"
"Oh, I am just heading down to the river to go for a run, what's up? How is the lake?"
"Well, the police called and I guess Dad has been in an accident somewhere. They have taken him to the hospital. But you go for your run and I will call you back once I see him."

Silence. But my brain starts running... my stomach tightens.

"Um, no. I will meet you at the hospital, Mom." I was thinking she was already in shock with the news because I could make no sense of why she wouldn't want me there.

I meet my mother at the hospital and we get in to see Dad. He is taped to a backboard. My heart starts pounding. My throat gets tight. I am trying to stay cool and supportive. Like, this is all going to be okay. Given that he already had a fused spine from a disease he has had since his early twenties (Ankylosing spondylitis – remember I ran my first marathon for arthritis), any injury to his neck or spine immediately puts him at considerable risk. I am almost scared to touch him. I can see he is in pain. I can see the worry in his face. This is not good.

He is conscious and he explains to me that he believes he has broken his neck. We are waiting for MRI's and CAT scans but he tells me, "I heard it snap. It's broken." With his spine already fused together, he didn't have the normal flexible spine assisting with the absorption of the impact. Instead the doctors explained, he had what was described as a brittle twig and upon impact his neck shattered like china.

The rest of the initial days in the hospital are just a blur. Conversations with doctors, test results, moving him from one kind of backboard to another for the various machines and test. Transferring him to another hospital when it becomes clear how severe his injuries are, the level of care he needs, and the surgery he is going to need if he can manage to survive this injury. Mom's friend comes to offer help and support. I leave several messages on my brother's and sister's cell phones. They are both out of the province and out of cell range on summer vacations. I am try-ing not to sound panic-stricken and I don't want to alarm them when they turn their phones on and see fifteen missed calls from my phone.

The neurologist and other doctors discuss the extent of Dad's injuries. I feel absolutely sick to my stomach. He is really broken. They do not know exactly what to do or how they might fix him, but they know they need to operate. They do not know if he will survive the surgery or if the surgery to repair what has been damaged will leave him par-alyzed. He has broken his neck. His spinal cord is miraculously NOT severed. They have to find a way to put him together again and try to find bone healthy and strong enough to hold him together. We discussed his options and agreed there are no other options. He needed the surgery. We were allowed to talk with him for a minute before they took him away. I got to tell him I loved him. I told him I would see him after surgery. I prayed that I would.

I remember the doctors telling us how difficult it would to be to intubate him. They told him he would feel like they were suffocating him. My Dad told them to get that tube down his throat regardless of how much he struggled. He told them they were not to stop. He struggled. They didn't stop. They came out to tell us what a fighter he was. I was happy he was in fighting mode. I know my Dad and fighting mode was going to pay huge dividends in this case.

Prior to his surgery, despite the injuries to his neck, he could still feel his toes and his fingers. After eight hours of surgery that consisted of removal and graphing of hipbone into his neck, and the insertion of a rod and several screws, they woke him to assess what he could and couldn't feel. It appeared that he had lost all feeling so they put him back under and completed the surgery somewhat puzzled by this change. They explained to us that it could either be from swelling or from damage to the spinal cord during the surgery. We needed to wait. We needed to pray.

He woke up a little while later and seemed to be getting some feeling back in his toes. Hope. There was hope he would regain some, if not all of his feeling, if he survived. More waiting.

I finally got in touch with my siblings and was able to let them know what was going on and get their input on my Dad's care. They were both on their way home.

Dad woke up in recovery and I had the chance to see him. He was confused and swollen. He was talking about being hired by an intelligence agency to look at satellite photographs and provide an expert opinion on what was going on. In reality, the satellite photographs he was showing me and talking about were the water stains on the hospital room ceiling.

I never thought of the Ironman race or training (you forgot about it, too, didn't you?) or anything else other than Dad's recovery, helping Mom, and trying to hold my own family together. My two young children were very worried about their grandpa. I was trying to prepare them and not scare them. There was endless waiting. The pain post surgery was unbearable for my dad. For several days he was in a drug-induced haze but as he became more alert we were relieved and amazed at his ability to withstand this much trauma. My father began his recovery by learning how to swallow, so he was not at all fooled by what it would take to regain his life and neither were we. He told me he could hear the bones in his neck moving. He wasn't sure his head was really "on" anymore. He feared choking. He didn't want to be left alone. This folks, is square one.

In the three weeks following my Dad's accident, I put on about fifteen pounds. I didn't train once, nor did I even think going to Ironman was even in the cards. Truth be told, as soon as I was aware how severely injured he was and that his life was on the line, I had resigned myself to doing it another time under different circumstances. I was totally okay with that. I had already laid that to rest. I knew his recovery would take a very long time.

But, Dad was being less and less medicated and one day, when he was able to wake up enough to speak in a manner I could understand, he asked me about Ironman. I told him I wasn't going. He asked me why (although it seemed obvious to me!). He told me he needed me to go to Ironman. He knew that I had worked hard and it would upset him to know I trained for a year and then his accident prevented me from seeing that dream come true. He told me it would mean a lot to him to watch me see it through. Mom and Dad were supposed to be at Ironman with my children and I. This is not what any of us had planned.

Yet, I could barely process his request. How could I go take part when he was laying there fighting for his life? I understood that it was important to him that I still go, that he felt like he didn't want his accident to keep me from something that I dreamed of doing but I didn't even want to go. I felt overwhelmed and I was filled with fear that I would be returning to bury him.

He was pretty insistent. It was important to him so it became important to me again. But I was really torn about leaving. Finally, we came to an agreement that I would go only if he used all the energy I put out on the Ironman course for his own recovery and rehabilitation, sort of like an energy credit card plan of some type. With the amount of metal holding him together, I deemed him an Ironman in his own right and started making plans to earn that title for myself by other means. I remember telling him he was in training for his life now. Recovering was his job now. That needed to be his focus.

Plan B was pulled together hastily and friends and family rallied to support me and to help me with my children on race day. I went and took part in the Ironman, my parents tracked me online, and cheered me across the finish line. While there is an entirely miraculous story to be told about my Dad's recovery, I just want to focus on his perception of these events and how it served his recovery and lifted people up all around him.

His Attitude
Not only did my father find a way to feel gratitude in his situation almost from the moment he ended up in the Emergency Room, but he didn't

drag anyone down to "ease" his pain. He convinced me to take part in Ironman when I had let go of it. He was the one who inspired me to go and do it! Had he had a "woe is me" or victim mindset he would likely have insisted I stay. Instead, he served as an inspiration to LIVE in the moment out there on the Ironman course. His positive attitude not only helped him in his remarkable recovery, it helped everyone around him too! (Yes, he had his down days and setbacks but overall he was positive.)

Recently, I asked him if he woke up thinking, "Why me?" and if he was filled with despair or gratitude. I wondered how long it took him to decide he was going to get better or if he had wanted to die? His answers made me really stop and think. My father never wanted to die but he wanted to escape the pain. Here is his take on his lowest moment.

"There was only one time that things became more than I could take and that was shortly after the surgery. The pain was so bad I couldn't see how I could endure it. I concluded in the middle of the night that my time had come, so I held my breath thinking that I could become unconscious and escape the pain – and drift – off. I held my breath until I lost consciousness – but then rather than "drifting – off" I regained consciousness sometime later! The nurse gave me a shot of painkiller and I concluded that I was 'doomed to live' – and never looked back!"

He explained to me that he doesn't remember ever feeling despair but he did feel incredibly blessed. When he was moved to the rehabilitation ward, he was with two young men who had spinal injuries and both were paraplegics. My father felt extreme gratitude, for at sixty-five, "here was the old guy with three fractured and one smashed vertebrae and a piece of his ass grafted into his neck, and he was walking down the hall!" He also clearly remembers being told by his physiotherapist that she was there to help him but **if he wasn't committed to his recovery,** nothing they could do would help in any meaningful way.

My dad has recovered almost completely from this accident but not without several setbacks. By Thanksgiving he was able to come in a wheelchair to my house for a family supper. He was walking (a few steps) again months later with assistance. He was able to return home and with some modifications to door handles and taps, can do everything for himself. It's been five years and I am still amazed.

Would you see things the same way if you found yourself in a similar situation? He made a deliberate choice to look for the blessings he had left and it gave him hope for his recovery. He focused on the good.

If you are sitting there thinking that you have a long journey ahead of you, I am here to tell you that ANYTHING is possible. I'd also like to point out, that there are many people who would love your life right now, just as it is, so make sure you do what you can to feed a healthy perspective and feel gratitude for what you DO have.

Remember, perspective is YOUR choice.

Cancer's Blessing

I watched an amazing video the other day about a young man named Zach Sobiech. The series from which this clip came from is entitled *MY LAST DAYS*. At fourteen Zach was diagnosed with cancer, yet he refused to just give up and die. In fact, his mother claims that there was, indeed, a blessing in his cancer diagnosis despite the fact that this sweet young man left us in May of 2013 at just eighteen. "With cancer you are forced to come out of denial," she explained. "The simple things in life are better and everything means more." You get to decide how your story is going to end, regardless of how dire your situation is and Zach lived this to his last days.

He chose to live his life big. He made a YouTube video about life, love, and living life fully. He used that video to leave a legacy. He loved his girlfriend and told her he would love her for the rest of his life. They made great memories in the time they had left. With only months to live, he used his musical talent to write a song called "Clouds" to say goodbye to everyone he loved so dearly. His song went viral, his message spread, and he inspired many people. He changed lives around the world with his inspirational message. Proceeds from the sale of "Clouds" go to fund research to help find a cure for this disease that claims the lives of many young people. He made a difference in the lives of so many people and he lived a life full of love.

Zach wanted everyone to know that "you don't have to wait until you are dying to begin to live your life with the meaning you deserve." In fact, it would be great if you didn't have to wait for any major life event such as divorce, loss, illness, or emotional trauma to begin living. Let us not forget Zach's message. If you need a lesson in perspective, please Google his video. And please remember, you do not need permission from anyone to live a rich and amazing life.

Denial Is Comfortable

I am often surprised how many people live in a state of denial. I shouldn't be because I used to call that place home too. Denial keeps you stuck. Living where you know all the rules is comfortable and predictable, even if you are not particularly happy there. Seeking happiness can bring lots of uncertainty but why is that always perceived as bad? Uncertainty can be "over the top" exciting! We tend to assume we have time to make the changes to make our life better, more fulfilling, and more balanced but the truth is, curve balls come out of nowhere and sometimes they happen as quickly as two cars colliding at an intersection. Time is not a given.

Denial and procrastination waste your life. We do not have to wait until tragedy strikes to change our lives but many of us feel that we don't have the permission to want something different and chase something different. It is like people with a tragedy have special permission to live a life that is richer because of what they have been through. Not so, live your life now. Now is all that you are guaranteed.

Carpe Diem

The vast majority of us regret not what we have done, but what we have NOT done. My teenage son reminded me of this lesson when we were on a mother–son trip to San Francisco over Canadian Thanksgiving. It was his thirteenth birthday gift, as I felt thirteen was an important age and I wanted to make memories and not just give him "things." I took him there to see Navy Fleet Week because he is a Sea Cadet in Canada and spends his summers on the coast of BC at cadet camps. He was fascinated. We wandered the wharf and he took me for dinner at a great crab restaurant (with the help of his grandfather) and we sat and talked and enjoyed the atmosphere of being somewhere new. He noticed earlier that you could rent bikes and ride across the Golden Gate Bridge. We both thought it would be fun. The following day, when we had "just enough time" to do it, I started making excuses (frankly, I was tired and we had only so much time to get across to the bike ferry pick up point to catch the last ferry of the day).

That sweet child of mine looked at me with his eyes all filled with excitement and said, "Look where we are! It took us a year to get here! Let's do this! When will we ever be here together again? Remember, Mom, people regret the things they do not do!" I knew he was right. We rented the bikes.

What a memory-maker that ride was. We biked quickly along the coast and up and over the bridge. We noticed red suicide hotline phones at every post, which led to a discussion every parent should have with a teenage child. We stopped to take in the view. We fought the wind up on the bridge and laughed because it was such a hard ride. Then we zipped down along the other side and giggled at confusing signage. We had NO IDEA where we were. We cycled past little shops and cafes.

The road was curvy and fun. We had an absolute blast! We arrived at the ferry with five minutes to spare and while we waited and caught our breath, we laughed more and more about what an experience that ride was.

Soon, we learned there had been a bomb threat at the ferry building so the ferry would not be running until that was sorted out. We had no option but to wait, along with others in the same situation. We made some new friends waiting in line and I was able to observe my son in a situation that made me feel so proud of the man he had become. What a gift that day was. This is one of my fondest memories of time spent with my son. I did not regret renting those bikes and I never will.

Just recently, he reminded me again when I was out visiting him at cadet camp. Now fifteen, I had not seen him for over a month and I flew in to pick him up for a day of leave. I mentioned I saw sea kayak rentals and asked if he wanted to maybe do that for half a day. He said, "Remember the bike ride?" and a big smile grew across his face. We rented the kayaks and for three hours we paddled and talked and laughed our way along the shoreline playing with sea lions and enjoying the baby pups trying to get up on logs while their mothers nudged them out of the ocean. Away from "real life," we had the chance to connect for a long period of time and to talk about the things that mattered most to both of us at the time. Because he had been away from home for over a month at this point, I craved time alone to connect. It is things like these that I cherish most, all done on a whim (we didn't even have sunscreen or water). Living in the NOW. Not waiting for a better time to have an experience but simply having it and surrendering to the joy it brings: Relishing the unknown.

Perspective is incredibly powerful.

Before and After: Thriving in a New Normal

While I have always been aware that people have limited time on earth, I never really considered that this "rule" applied to my family too. And neither do you, right? I mean we all have this sense that we are somewhat invincible, or that something horrible can't happen to me because (insert why you are special/different here). But, then my father had his car accident and my twelve-year-old daughter developed a neurological disorder the year I turned forty. I went from being able to say to the kids, "Hey, I will be home in an hour, make yourself something to eat and don't fight" to not being able to leave my daughter in a room alone. I slept with her out of fear I wouldn't be there to help her in the night if she needed me.

I realized I needed help to establish a long-term, sustainable, new normal, so I could do things like go get groceries without fearing my daughter would die while I was away. My mindset had shifted dramatically because of an experience I will explain shortly. I was left traumatized by what I had seen. My fear was out of control. I was incredibly anxious. And, I knew better!

Some events push you from your current life, providing an unplanned exit from a situation, a way of thinking, or a lifestyle. But if you are ever forced to exit one life, you have no option but to walk through an entrance to another. Events happen in our lives that forever divide our lives into a before and an after. "After the accident..." or "After the divorce..." or "Before I lost him..." Your life changes as a result. It could be marriage, birth of children, a diagnosis, divorce, an accident, or a traumatic event. Really, the only question left to ask is, "What will the new normal be like?"

On December 31, around noon I jumped into the shower. My friend Jim was in the kitchen. My daughter (then twelve) had had a friend for a sleepover the previous night and the girls were eating their breakfast and watching TV. Everything was as it should be.

All of a sudden, there was a banging on the bathroom door. I couldn't hear what was being said but there was definitely a sense of urgency to the commotion. I was covered in shampoo but I turned the water off and heard my daughter's friend yelling that something was wrong with my daughter.

I flew from the shower covered in soap and grabbed a towel on my way out of the bathroom. I ran into the living room to find Jim kneeling next to my daughter on the floor. My world stopped. I could only see her pajama bottoms and her feet. I moved forward with my eyes squeezed shut because he looked panic-stricken and I was terrified of what I was going to see. I opened my eyes to find my daughter laying there with her eyes partially open and rolled back in her head. Her face was completely grey. She was foaming at the mouth and her arms were twisted and contorted into her chest. She was moving spastically. Most alarming was that there was no breath escaping her sweet lips. Her color was so disturbing to me and my mind took off running. "Oh my God, that's what dead people look like! She isn't dead! She isn't dead! Oh my God, she is dead! Noooo! Oh my baby! Oh my GOD! No! No!"

I remember vividly that I could hear the blood rushing through my ears, time slowed to a complete crawl as I reached for the phone to call 911. Her friend stood in the corner watching all of this play out, and I had forgotten she was even in the room. I partially covered myself while I knelt down next to my daughter with the 911 operator on the line trying to determine whether my child was breathing or not.

She was not breathing. She was grey. She was not responding. It was the most horrifying thing I have ever seen and I felt utterly helpless. Her convulsions stopped and she stilled completely. I watched her and willed her to breathe. I was talking to God and BEGGING her to breathe, BEGGING for this not to be happening, and BEGGING for this to not be our end. Jim had rolled my daughter into the recovery position and the saliva rolled from her still lips. I watched intently for breath. Her lips were silent. Time stood absolutely still.

And then, she took a very shallow breath. And, another. And, another. I waited for her to open her eyes and recognize me. I wasn't sure exactly how long she had been without oxygen and I was worried her brain had been damaged. She opened her eyes but was confused and she drifted in and out of consciousness. Her eyes were unrecognizable because her pupils had overtaken her blue eyes completely. The ambulance arrived and we went to the hospital. Unbeknownst to me at the time, I would be spending a lot of time there with my daughter over the coming years.

I have never experienced anything like that moment. The image of my little girl contorted and struggling to breathe burned itself into the back of my eyelids. Every time I shut my eyes, I would see her like that. No matter what I did, I couldn't blink that image away. It fed my greatest fear.

I had such incredible anxiety about leaving her alone. Just when I had relaxed a little bit and was giving her a little more room to breathe, she had another seizure three weeks later. Clearly something was going on that we couldn't identify. There were more seizures and my anxiety was at an all-time high. I kept thinking what if she has a seizure and doesn't start breathing again? What if she is alone? Her seizures were creating a belief that my daughter could not be left alone because if she had a seizure she would die. I could feel this belief beginning to take control and it was choking me. I knew I was in trouble.

Medically, we investigated from all angles as she continued to have more seizures: MRI's, CAT Scans, EEG's, blood tests, medications, neurologists, pediatricians, dieticians, naturopathic doctors, chiropractors, and energy healers. I was digging in. I hired a nanny so I could do some of the simple things like get groceries, grab a haircut, or meet a client. She was so sleepy from the medication, dragging her along with me wasn't an option. Leaving her with her brother didn't seem fair, either, should the unimaginable happen. She wasn't at all impressed to have a babysitter when she used to be one.

Life before her seizures and life after: I felt like I had a small child who needed constant tending. My freedom and her independence both vanished. Life changed. We have both had to adjust to a new normal. I have worked hard to move through the fear of losing this child to something that has no explanation. Whenever I cannot get a hold of her or she tells me she feels ill, I have to wrestle with that fear inside me that something bad is going to happen to her.

Two unexplained seizures and you get a diagnosis of Epilepsy. We do not know the cause of her seizures. Epilepsy and my incredible daughter have taught me some big lessons. First of all, I have learned that death can visit you anywhere and that in all honestly, it is simply an injury or a few breaths away for all of us. **None of us really plan to die. The funny thing is that many of us do not plan to live either.** We just move through life, doing countless things that mean little to us. If we knew that we had four weeks to live or an hour, how differently might that change our perspective on how we spend our time and energy? Really chew on that one. What would you do differently? Why are you not doing that now?

The second thing is the value of humor and a light heart. While I myself have always tried to find the humor in bad situations, I have never seen that practiced from the outside looking in. I watched my daughter as we moved through the unknown together. I saw the apprehension on her face before big test days, EEGs, or doctor visits. I heard her concern and felt her own fear when she asked the hard questions. We would sit together waiting, holding hands, sometimes her head in my lap as she stretched out to relax. Out of the blue she would say something so incredibly inappropriate and funny and we would both crumple into stifled giggles. One day as we were discussing some things we needed to do, I was telling her that she needed to get a mole removed. She looked at me all puzzled, when suddenly she smirked and broke into song and dance while pointing to her mole, "This is a part of me that you're never ever gonna take away from me." (Katy Perry's hit song, "Part of Me"). The mere act of laughing and taking a few deep breaths cut the tension from our bodies and helped us deal with the most stressful of times. She was a pro at this, right down to playfully imitating the doctor (in his presence, I might add) while staring at me with laughter in her eyes, daring me to lose my composure. Anyone who knows this dear child of mine, knows her sense of humor. She kept it light.

Thirdly, I learned to depend on gratitude. Since we were unsure of what was causing the seizures, each new one told me we still had work to do. We are two years out and she is still not controlled. I was thankful to see that their duration was decreasing. When we got a clear MRI, I was thankful that there wasn't a mass growing into her brain that would need to be removed. I was thankful I was on educational leave the year she got sick so that my focus could be entirely on her wellness. I was so incredibly grateful for each day that was seizure free. We celebrated her good days and every baby step. I was appreciative of my friends' and family's support. I was glad that she was moving through the medical system quickly. I was grateful that no seizure had caused any permanent damage. When I focused on the good things happening around us, it made managing the bad stuff easier. Gratitude helped me gain some control over my fears of the unknown. Gratitude – encouraged me to enjoy NOW. It took my focus off the shitty, heartbreaking stuff and directed my focus to all that was good.

Finally, my daughter fought me hard to regain her independence. There were some moments of intense conflict. I was terrified to let her out of my sight. At first, going to another room for a few minutes was all I could muster. When I felt like I was making headway, we would have setbacks. A plate would hit the floor followed by absolute silence and I would know even before arriving in the room that I would find her seizing. I would be back to arguing with her and my common sense about what she could and couldn't do. The cold hard truth was that even if I put her in a bubble wrapped box, it wouldn't stop the seizures, but her life was still moving on and I was in the way!

My daughter told me that I had to stop being afraid. She needed to be a kid. I tried with all my heart to respect this and we negotiated rules as her health improved. I loved her spirit. I loved that she wasn't paralyzed by fear. While she felt it I am sure, she never surrendered to it. She never fed it. In fact, she even told me once that she "didn't care" if she had seizures. She had no memory of them. It was just a severe headache and a long nap for her. When she shared that with me, I realized that my experience of her seizures was vastly different from her own. I knew I had to face my fears because they were suffocating her.

Quite honestly, this was the hardest thing to do. But I let go of everything I couldn't control and I knew that if her time ever came, I would do everything in my power to keep her safe and alive. I updated my first aid and CPR. I came to terms with the understanding that I had no control over her time on earth (or my own or my son's for that matter) and that I had to let her LIVE her life and not smoother it out of her with my fear. Her words and wisdom allowed me to move forward.

I couldn't live my daughter's life for her and while she had no idea how this entire experience had impacted my life, I didn't have a full understanding of how it impacted hers either. I knew she had to regain responsibility for her own life and how she would chose to live it and I didn't need to disable her by projecting my fears on her. She was game.

She WANTED the responsibility. She needed it. On the flip side, she wasn't responsible for my anxiety and fears and it was up to me to sort out that crap on my own. Together, we worked to find a new normal that worked for both of us so we could both THRIVE in our new normal while regaining independence, freedom and doing what we could to keep her safe and me sane.

I'm Not Just Blowing Smoke

Dr. Dweck is a leading researcher in the field of motivation and a renowned Professor at Stanford University. She has spent years exploring the impact that specific mindsets can have on our lives. In her book, *Mindset: The New Psychology of Success - How We Can Learn to Fulfill Our Potential*, she looks specifically at two mindsets: the "growth mindset" and the "fixed mindset." In the growth mindset, people embrace change and challenge because they understand that life begins outside your comfort zones. In the fixed mindset, failure is to be avoided at all cost because it becomes a reflection of your self worth. In this mindset, Dwerk said people believe their "personal qualities are carved in stone" so they need to prove their worth over and over. If they stumble, it impacts their self worth. In other words, the fixed mindset believes that people are born with all the talent, intelligence, and personality characteristics you will ever possess. Furthermore, fixed mindsets focuses on the outcome alone so if you fail, time spent working towards something is wasted. People in a fixed mindset never examine a situation for the learning it offers. Even more troublesome is that people who function in a fixed mindset tend to exert much less effort. I mean, why bother if you are born as good as you are going to get! Whoa! That's a limiting mindset!

On the flipside, Dwerk says the growth mindset comes from a place of believing "that the hand you are dealt is just the starting point for development. The growth mindset believes that your basic qualities are things you can cultivate through your efforts... that everyone can change and grow through application and experience." People operating from a growth mindset also are not just focused on the out-come, but they are enthusiastic and passionate about what they are doing and that passion helps them succeed. If they fail, they look for lessons. If they succeed, they look for lessons. They understand that if they continue to stretch themselves and put forth the effort and do the work, they can actually thrive during the most challenging times of their lives because they can convert setbacks into future successes. Failure isn't the end of the world. Failure is a lesson or an opportunity to wake up (a WTF Moment).

All of this is great news for you because you are no slouch if you are already reading a book about "creating" a life you love. You are pre-pared to DO the work and find your passion--you just need a little guidance! If by chance you have realized you have lived in a fixed mind-set, that's okay, too, because while mindsets are powerful beliefs bouncing around in your head, they can be changed! Your potential is UNKNOWN. So roll up your sleeves and get ready to DO THE WORK.

Dweck's research has demonstrated clearly that the mindset you adopt will make a HUGE impact on the quality of your life and your happi-ness. "Your mindset can determine whether you become the person you want to be and whether you accomplish things that you value." Kinda seals the deal in my books, what about yours?

What am I trying to tell you?

You have no promises of your life being eighty years long or even twenty! You are running out of time as you read this book. Everything you do consumes some of your time here on earth. Don't you want to use your energy and your time to create something unbelievably and wonderfully blissful? Instead of just living, don't you want to feel ALIVE? At eighteen, even Zach could identify that most people live their lives where it is comfortable. **Do you want to be comfortable or do you want to be excited, inspired, and engaged fully in your**

life? Zach wanted to be remembered as "the kid who went down fighting and who didn't really lose." I think he made his point. Be engaged in YOUR OWN life now! Get out there and play along the edges!

SWIFTKICK TIP: Coping with Crisis with "The Box"

Curve balls happen and when they do, your stress load can be out-of-this-world heavy. This is a strategy I learned about when training for Ironman in 2008 from an article I read called, The Endurance Nation "Four Keys" To Ironman Execution. (http://www.trifuel.com/training/ triathlon-training/the-endurance-nation-four-keys-to-ironman-exe-cution#.UgQVHxZAza4). I know, I know, you are thinking what the hell does triathlon race execution have to do with coping with crisis but this strategy has saved my ass on numerous occasions, including my dad's accident and my daughter's sudden illness, and it would have been very helpful while going through my divorce and infertility treatments, so listen up.

The authors of this article talk about The Box. The Box is defined as a space where you can control everything while you race (or live) with the goal or idea that by dealing with only the things you can control NOW, you avoid looking too far off into the future and worrying about stuff you cannot control. For example, in the swim portion of the race, "the box is the space your body occupies in the water: focus on the form and the rest will come. On the bike, the box is probably one aid station long. On the run, the box begins as 2-3 aid stations long but often diminishes to from here to the next lamp post/manhole." The rules for creating your own box are as follows:

1. Only things you can control are allowed in the box. Let go of everything else. (In the case of my dad's accident, that box was really small (sixty seconds). We concerned ourselves ONLY with what we could control in the next minute. This kept us from hitting the panic button and starting with "What if he doesn't

make it?" "What if he does and he can't walk or feed himself?" "What if, what if, what if?"

2. Keep the box as large as you can for as long as you can. Shrink the box when it is hitting the fan and enlarge it when things seem to lift up a bit. (In the case of my daughter's seizures, the box could get considerably bigger when it had been days since her last seizure. That box shrunk really quickly when she started having grand mal seizures close together and I was alone with her. I shrunk the box to thirty seconds, as I did what I could in that half a minute, then moved on to the next thirty seconds.)

3. When you are inside the box, you use a decision-making process called OODA Loop. You OBSERVE the situation, you ORIENT yourself to possible course of actions, you DECIDE on the best course of action, and finally you ACT. No humming and hawing the heck out of things, you move!

What this strategy does is it keeps you firmly planted in NOW. This allows you to focus your energy on what you need to deal with NOW, not what "might happen." Imagine if you spend valuable energy focusing on what might happen, so much so, you have no energy to focus on now and what is happening. Just a quick illustration, when my father had his accident, my siblings were both in remote "off the grid" locations. I met Mom at the ER and it become clear pretty quickly, we were going to be making some life altering decisions in the very near future. I will spare you the medical details, but surgery was the only option and the outcome uncertain. In that thirty-second box, Mom, Dad, and I prepared for his surgery. In another thirty-second box, I had a few words with my dad and told him I loved him. In the next thirty- second box, he was off to surgery. Now of course I was wondering what was going on in the OR and how he was doing, but THAT was out of my control short of praying with every breath I took. However, what was in my control was trying to contact my siblings again and trying to keep my mom from losing her mind by running off into the unknown future hunting down "what ifs" to worry about. My box got a little bigger and I was making calls and trying to track them down and taking care of Mom (and getting her in her own box) with help from her good friend. Post op, they told us that he couldn't feel his feet. Box shrinks. What do we need to do? What does he need from us? Let's do it. Hours later, he CAN feel his toes. Box increases a wee bit as he is still in precarious times but we celebrate that progress. Siblings get in touch. Box gets a bit bigger. You get the drift of how this works I am sure.

This strategy has served me very well and it really supports you in times of crisis. And yes, it helps you execute a great Ironman race too!

SWIFTKICK TIP: Change Your Perspective and Let Your Perspective Change You

Your life might truly suck right now. I am going to make you hate me and remind you that it always could be worse. Really, it could. Someone's Facebook post drifted across my wall the other day, complaining about the rain that was never-ending. She sounded like she was going to die. She had used language that totally over dramatized the impact this rain had on her life.

I thought to myself, "Go dance in the rain, silly. Make the most of this rainy day by changing your focus! Spend the time inside doing something that you wanted to get done anyway. Clean a closet, catch up on laundry, call a friend, or prepare some healthy meals because it is a great day for that!"

One summer day when it was raining nonstop here in Saskatoon, my daughter was resting in her bed complaining about how bored she was while she surfed the Internet mindlessly. So I told her to get up and get some grubby clothes on, we were going outside to play.

"What are we doing? What do you mean, play?"

Really I had no idea. No Plan. I constructed it as I spoke. "We are going to go down to the river and do a mud scramble."

"What the heck is that?" She was getting excited and I could sense it in her voice.

"We are going to run in the rain and through puddles and we are going to get muddy and laugh and have fun!" Her eyes lit up!

To this day, when I talk about that mud scramble, my daughter smiles and talks about how awesome it was. We laughed and slipped and stumbled our way through mud puddles. She grabbed handfuls of earthworms from murky puddles and chased me across the riverbank laughing from the deepest parts of her heart. We created a great day because we decided that was exactly what we were going to do! That rainy day is one of my most cherished memories with my daughter.

Perspective is a choice. So if you can't eliminate the things that drive you nuts, change your take on them. Use gratitude to appreciate what you DO have, not what you feel you are missing. Focus on the good until all you see is good. Don't be a wet blanket and ooze depression into the lives of your friends and family. Be the one who offers an uplifting perspective and energizes a room.

If you are feeling overwhelmed right now by the weight of your worries and your situation, make a list of three things you are grateful for and if you are really grasping, I might suggest that merely breathing is something to be grateful for if you can't seem to find anything else. If you are really drowning in negativity, you may feel some resistance to this because it feels GOOD. Sometimes we continue to gravitate to what we know because it is comfortable, and if you have had a lengthy "bad run" feeling good can be uncomfortable, foreign, and even down right scary.

Feeling good can make you feel guilty. You might even push it away. Denise Duffield-Thomas, best-selling author of *Lucky Bitch: A Guide for Exceptional Women to Create Outrageous Success*, talks about how she "knew she had to increase her capacity for pleasure in order to receive this massive opportunity (her dream job) and believe that she deserved it." In fact, she even discusses how increasing your pleasure threshold is a way to increase your over-all self-care. It is okay to feel good. It is even more okay to feel downright splendid! **Stay with it, practice gratitude on a daily basis, and this one habit will change your entire life.**

Ladies, we are well on our way but we still have more to talk about. Maybe your drink needs a refill? So far we have examined the power of a WTF Moment and the importance of accepting responsibility for your own life. Through some personal stories about life's curve balls, we have learned the importance of your perspective and perception on how you deal with whatever is tossed your way.

But how do we actually create a life we love?

PART 3:
Creating Your Plan for Change

The clearer you become the easier the rest of this process will be. I promise. Clarity brings ease, confidence, and a way of understanding what needs to be done and how to do it.

Having discussed the concept of a WTF Moment and examining the importance of perspective (mindset), we now move on to explore how you can go about putting together a plan that supports you in making the changes you seek.

This plan begins with understanding that unless you are in a state of awareness, things happen anyway, just without your input. I'll introduce you to a little love-hate triangle between default systems, limiting or supporting beliefs, and awareness. Once you understand how these things work together (or in conflict) you will be highly motivated to get clear about what you want without the outside world influencing your choices! You will learn how to be true to yourself, let go of things that hold you back, face your fears, make powerful decisions, and learn how to follow through with actionable plans!

Let's take things up a notch now and learn a little "somethang somethang" about getting off!

Chapter 4:
IT'S TIME TO GET OFF

I know I got you all excited, sorry. This isn't about what you think it is but getting off default mode is even MORE amazing than what your dirty little mind was thinking I was going to talk about.

As humans, we all have default settings, which dictate how we function day to day. The default settings don't require any conscious thought to run. They get you out of bed, selecting clothes to wear, brushing your teeth, eating your breakfast, and heading out the door. You do all of these things without even really thinking about them. They are somewhat automatic. Ever arrive at home after a long day and not remember any part of the drive? Say hello to Default.

Your default system is much like the operating system of a computer and it just runs quietly in the background. However, your default system is influenced by your belief system, and your belief system also runs quietly in your head making sure to keep your default behaviors inline with your internal belief system. These two systems have an intricate little love affair. The belief system more or less tells the default system what and how to do things. The default system's job is to just do and never ask why. The default system is unaware.

If we look at a specific default-setting behavior like getting dressed, for example, the default system has you getting up and mindlessly picking out some clothes to wear. But the belief system is watching over everything and it sees you leaning towards that blue top you just bought because you felt so pretty in it. Just as you reach for it, the belief system whispers to the default system, *"She doesn't really deserve to feel pretty, and she is a little on the chunky side so maybe try that black top over there because it will thin her out a bit...."* Default just does as it is told, and the blue shirt stays in the closet unworn. It's a subtle affair, but it almost seems abusive. The belief system can be a serious bitch, especially if your beliefs are negative and limiting. She is sneaky and she will weave her threads through every part of your being. The default system has been beaten into submission and it would never even consider taking a stand. As long as these two keep up their dance, you have no real chance of anything different. So if you are going to shift this dynamic and start breaking cycles that don't serve you, you have to introduce a new player. Lucky for you, I know just what you need. Girlfriend, I would like for you to meet Awareness.

A Bizarre Love Triangle: Default Mode, Beliefs, and Awareness

Maybe you are like I was. For many years I just woke up, did what needed to be done, and went to bed. Period. Default ran my whole life (with my limiting belief system keeping everything in check). I was just doing what needed to be done. My actions and behaviors were a direct reflection of my inner belief systems and it was clear I felt unworthy of anything better. Deep down, I felt that I was a bad person and that happiness wasn't something I deserved.

It wasn't that I didn't enjoy being a mom or that I totally hated my job as a teacher, it was that I had no direction, no goals, and no defined purpose. I had NO sense of awareness. I had NO clarity about what I really wanted.

"If you do not know where you are going, any road will do." Unknown

I was wishy-washy in my decision making because I wasn't really clear about what I wanted or even what I thought I believed in anymore. "Should we do this or that?" It didn't matter because I had no idea where I was going. My default settings or my "auto-pilot" mode seemed to be just "do what needs to be done." Half the time I didn't even know why I was doing what I was doing. It must have been on "someone's" to-do list, maybe, if I was lucky, it was actually on mine.

I was also mentally exhausted and had no time or energy to think on my own for just a few minutes. I never had the chance to get clear, and back then even if I had the time, I wouldn't have known what it meant to "get clear." In fact, terms like getting clear, setting intentions, or finding my calling would have set off my "woo-woo" radar and anyone speaking to me using such terms would have been classified immediately as a nut job. So, if you are thinking I am a nut job, hey, I have been there and I completely understand. But it is the nut jobs that actually change the world so grab a nut job flag and let's do this together!

Awareness Arrives

After my glorious WTF Moment, things started changing because I suddenly became more AWARE of everything around me. Instead of letting life happen TO me, I started asking questions, "Why am I doing this?" "What is this doing for me?" and Awareness pointed its finger at my Default Behaviors and asked, "Why have you been letting me live my life like this for so long?"

And then I realized I needed to be pointing my finger at myself (Awareness) asking, "Why the hell have you let Default run your life without asking a few questions?" Look at the mess you have gotten yourself into. Girlfriend, it is time to get the hell off of default! It is time to start stepping up and taking back a little control.

A separation and ultimately a divorce was a by-product of my initial WTF Moment and a partial solution to taking back control of my own life. It was part of letting go and moving forward so I could focus on my wellness. So, by this point I was a single parent and I was still getting used to solo flight. I had the kids much of the time and I always had things to do to keep me busy. Busy as in, "I have no time to think about this stuff that is nagging at me beneath the surface," until one day I was alone, in an empty house, without the kids and without a to-do list in my hands.

Awareness had arrived and it started stirring the pot. I was good at staying busy (not to be mistaken for being productive) but my clutter wasn't serving the new life I wanted; in fact, it only continued to serve the person I used to be. All this mindset clutter was stockpiled beneath the surface and it was going to keep me stuck where I didn't want to be anymore. All this stuff, all these mixed messages, and all these limiting beliefs ... ALL of it had to go.

I knew it was time to "get off" autopilot and I was afraid. I had so many questions to ask myself. I had endless things I knew I needed to change. If I was ever going to live my life with a sense of purpose and direction, I knew I would have to turn parts of it upside down.

I was overwhelmed. I made lists of what I thought I needed to do and then I made more lists. How was I ever going to be able to figure this out? How would I ever find the time to get done what needed to get done?

In that quiet house, Awareness finally got beneath my busy-ness and numbness and every other single defense mechanism I had erected to protect myself from the pain I felt. I finally broke. I cried and cried and cried. The silence in the house swallowed me whole. I fell asleep exhausted but I woke up and I made a new list that changed everything.

SWIFTKICK TIP: Start with Stopping

Okay, if you did the activities in the previous SWIFTKICK TIPS, you have had a little reality check. You now have a good idea how much room you have for a happiness improvement plan. You know in your gut what events and behaviors have gotten you to where you currently stand. You may have even started to identify areas where your default and belief systems have been messing with your progress.

Grab the free journal that goes with this book from www.swiftkickfitness.com because we have more work to do! Right now you are going to make a list that is going to lighten your load, streamline your focus, and make a huge difference about how you feel about where you currently are in your life. We are going to start with stopping. We are going to increase your awareness about how your actions impact your results. We are taking you off of autopilot and kicking default to the curb. Boo yah!

Yes, I can hear the panic in your voice, "Huh, are you for real?" Yes, I can hear your inside voice screaming, "But I have 'stuff' to do! I have to get going! I don't have time for this!"

Let me explain. (And if you don't like it, blame my brother because he re-introduced me to this concept a few years back. Hell ya, I come from a family of enlightened peeps!)

Sometimes our inability to focus on our goals or what appears as a lack of commitment to our goals is a result of feeling incredibly overwhelmed by what we have to do, achieve, secure, create, and all of our to-do lists. So we are going to start with removing a few variables from this game.

We are going to create a Stopping List as a way to construct a day that is a little more in tune with what you desire to achieve. We want more of your focus on what you want and less on what robs you of precious time and focus.

Here is what I want you to do. Make a list of all the things you do in a given day from the moment you wake up until you go to bed, including the time periods you spend on Facebook, watching TV, small talk, or killing time. Do this for about three days unless weekend life is considerably different and if it is, do this time journaling for a week. Essentially, you are keeping a time journal, which is much like a food journal in that it is going to make you very aware about how you spend your time and what you spend your time doing.

Now you are going to write out your top goal or intention. This is going to be a big picture goal/intention. For example, you may wish to focus on your wellness by eating better, sleeping better, and integrating physical fitness into your daily life. Whatever it is, it must be YOUR intention. Own it. Write it in the box.

With your time journal in hand (please do not judge yourself for any behaviors you see that you want to criticize yourself for) and your intentions clearly defined, grab a highlighter and go through your time journal and highlight everything that DOES NOT serve your goals or intentions.

Now make a list on a new page and call it STOPPING LIST. Write down all of the behaviors you highlighted.

For example:

- Stop spending two hours a day on Facebook (Consider instead using a timer to allow yourself twenty minutes a day);
- Stop watching TV (Or consider allowing yourself to watch it one night a week so you can pick your favorite show; or allow yourself to only watch it if you are doing a workout at the same time).
- Stop the mindless eating and snacking after supper.

This is not about depriving yourself of the things you enjoy; it is about managing them and getting rid of anything that will not take you to your goals. It will help you streamline, gain time, increase focus, and start acting on what WILL take you where you need to go!

A list is still a list so make this one actionable. Once you have made your stopping list, you work towards actually STOPPING what is on it. Scribble some reminders into your day planner, set the phone to ping after your allotted Facebook time is up, put sticky notes on your walls and mirrors, remove the cable from your TV so when you sit down and turn it on mindlessly and it doesn't work, you are reminded WHY it doesn't work. Little tricks like this kick you off autopilot and keep you from falling into common habits and procedures that do not serve your new intentions.

Regardless of the bad habits, behaviors, and mindsets that have gotten you to where you currently are, KNOW that in order for things to change, YOU must change. Instead of adding more things to do, take away some things and stop doing the things that keep you stuck. The difference is subtle but the impact is huge. Tweet me a few of the items on your stopping list at @SwiftKickFitnes. I'd love to hear from you.

Chapter 5:
CLARITY - WHAT DO YOU REALLY WANT?

The more clear you can become about WHO you are and what exactly it is YOU want from your life, the more powerfully you can apply focus to direct your energy to achieving all you dream about. But first you have to be real. There are many capable women out there doing a great job at something that they feel no passion for because they serve the expectations someone else held for them. On the flipside, there are women out there who have dug deep and found their true passions and followed them with all the energy they could muster. The decision to truly live from a point of passion has created a more effortless and abundant life than merely existing in a life someone else might have planned for them.

Be Clear

The bottom line is that you have to be clear about what YOU want. You have to really dig deep and go inside your mind and heart. What does it feel like when you dream a certain dream? You know intuitively what feels right. We just have to shut up and quiet ourselves long enough to hear it and to feel it. We need to stop changing diapers and loading the dishwasher for a minute so we can focus on the task of thinking about and feeling what WE want.

Next, we have to have faith in ourselves and allow these dreams to grow and flourish in a way that allows us to be true to our own life's purpose. We need to be aware of where our dreams end - and the expectations, desires, or plans others might have for us - begin.

Yes, you will disappoint people but they WILL get over it. If they don't, that is not something you can control, so let it go. As Christine Kane, President and Founder of Uplevel You, teaches, allowing people their disappointment sets you free and it doesn't allow you to use another person's disappointment in you as an excuse to not live YOUR life.

Get clear. Dig deep. Discover your passions. Flip over rocks. Dissect your behaviors. Examine your beliefs. DREAM. Test your limits. Let go of things that need to go. Focus on all that is already good in your life and keep focusing on that until everything is good. Be grateful. Ask yourself HARD questions and stick around and ANSWER them. Invite struggle and reflection into your life to get clear. It is totally worth it!

No Pussyfoot'n

Nobody else can change your life. And if you allow other people to make choices for you, you will NOT be authentic, nor will you be connected to a purpose. If you aren't making your own decisions, you have given away your personal power. This is not about "control freak power," this is about the power you need to have to be able to access your authenticity. As soon as you can get clear, making life-changing decisions becomes so much easier!

You have to be tough, dig in, and stick it out until you can verbalize it and it feels good in your heart. Be tough on yourself now because clarifying your intentions determines your direction!

The clearer you become the easier the rest of this process will be. I promise. Clarity brings ease, confidence, and a way of understanding what needs to be done and how to do it.

Directions Only Help If You Know Where You Are Going

Here is a little story to demonstrate how clarity helps you focus and fine tune your energy expenditures to make your dreams come true!

Let's say you start your car and back out of your driveway so that you can head to the ... Wait a minute? You don't know where you are going! What do you do now? Maybe you can drive around and around the block for a little while until you figure it out or until someone else (very scary) tells you where you are supposed to be going?

Sounds kind of silly when it is put that way, doesn't it? Yet, how many of us really take the time to figure out where exactly we are heading before we start up the car? Even if you said, "I am going to go downtown," you still do not have the specifics and you might get downtown with no issue at all but then you may not know what to do or where to go when you get there! So you will be driving around and around downtown just like you were at home! What a waste of time and energy!

But if you knew you were headed to d'Lish by Tish Café on the corner of 14th at 2 p.m. to have coffee and a slice of the best carrot cake EVER with your sister, the chances of you getting there, on time, for the purpose of cake and a coffee is exponentially increased! When we take the above story and apply it to creating intentions/ vision/ goals, it is quickly apparent why knowing where you want to go is KEY to successfully getting exactly where you want to go!

We call this GETTING CLEAR! If you can get clear about your intentions, you can eliminate obstacles with EASE because if things are not in line with your intentions, they are released. There is no "wishy washy sorta" decision-making when you are CLEAR – you know what stays and more importantly you know what needs to go! When you realize something or someone is an obstacle to what you truly want, it is much easier to let go! In fact, it feels downright fabulous!

You Can't Please Everyone, So Please Yourself First

One day my sister and I took our four little ones to the zoo. Young mothers, managing the "supermom balance we can do it all syndrome" the best we could, our zoo trip was a chance to grab a coffee and catch up. We stopped at the goat enclosure and watched as the mom goat wandered around the corral and tried to avoid her kids. The baby goats found her and soon were suckling away madly. My sister and I leaned over the fence watching intently in silence, both of us feeling somewhat sympathetic. One kid moved to the left and pulled hard to take the nipple with it, the other kid moved to the right and fought to keep that nipple in its mouth too. Neither kid released momma goat's nipples and they continued to move and jostle to suckle "their nipple" on their terms.

Momma goat looked like she was sick of this nipple tug-o-war. She stood her ground, and as a result, had her two nipples being pulled aggressively in opposite directions for a few moments. My sister and I tensed over the fence, watching with a grimace to see how this might play out. Something had to give, nipples or kids. Right now it was a draw.

Neither baby goat was satisfied with their position or nipple output. Momma goat was being pulled in two directions. Clearly, it is hard to please each goat when they both have their own ideas about how things should be. Momma goat had her own ideas, too. I think she was fed up. She started backing up, stretching the distance and her nipples between each kid. My sister and I stiffened. (Ever have a nursing baby turn its head to watch something and take your nipple with it? Ya, you know what I mean!)

Eventually, the nipples snapped out of the kids' mouths, first the left one and then the right one. Mom stumbled to get her footing as the release of the nipples broke the tension between the kids and herself. Two stretched-out, saggy nipples hung from her, so misshapen they almost touched the ground beneath her. Slowly, her nipples recoiled back to their regular position and size. In complete silence, with our mouths open in amazement, my sister and I watched as her nipples took their proper place beneath her. The kids ran off to play and momma goat went off to eat alone in silence.

The moral of this story is simple. It is impossible to please everyone all of the time, so please yourself first. Make sure when you are getting clear about what YOU want, you are making sure that your needs are considered first. It is YOUR life. The baby goats can figure out how to get milk another way if their tug-o-war approach doesn't work! Are We Clear?

Sounds Easy. But what does it really mean?

- Getting clear means that you know who you are and why you do what you do. You are aware.
- When you are clear, you hold to your intentions even when others (or outside factors) try to derail you. Doing so makes you stronger. You understand the power in authenticity.
- When you are clear, you say NO to anything that isn't in line with your intentions. (If you have trouble with saying NO, check out the section on scripts).
- When you are clear, and you say NO to others, you understand you are saying YES to YOU!
- When you are clear you never apologize for WHO you are. You take risks and mess up and you apologize, without fear, for any mistakes you have made.

Sounds Like Work

Is it work initially to get clear? Absolutely. To dig deep into who you are and to be able to write out your intentions can be a struggle. But, once you have this nailed the rest becomes increasingly easy. Once you are clear on who you are and why you do what you do, you can LEVERAGE this knowledge to make every decision easier and to take the guess work out of actions you must take to get where you need to be! Having this clarity in your pocket means you stop spending valuable energy on things that don't serve you. Clarity is Queen!

Gaining clarity means that you are aware at every moment (that is the goal) and because you are aware of what is in your life and why it is there, you are not slipping into any form of automation or default setting, and you stop making decisions that are in conflict with your intentions. When you are distracted by all the things that are in conflict with your intentions, you are wasting your precious daily allowance of energy on things that DO NOT MATTER and that are going to do NOTHING to move you CLOSER to your INTENTIONS. **Clarity matters. Once you have got that, the rest falls into place.**

"One clear prayer beats a confused Cathedral any day." Unknown

The World is FULL of Confused People

If being clear can overhaul your life, you would think that everyone would BE CLEAR! However, as humans we are complex beings who also want to please others, be liked and accepted, or fit into social groups or situations. We are notorious for finding a comfortable holding pattern and then stagnating there. Sometimes we don't dislike where we are enough to start a movement out of that place. And, we are scared.

We are scared of making bad decisions. Scared of taking control for our lives and responsibility for our choices. Scared of digging deep to discover what belief systems have been running our show. Scared of learning we have not been true to ourselves and that we have been living a life planned by someone else because we let it happen.

AND, scared of our OWN GREATNESS. I am serious; once you start to get clear you will feel this incredible energizing sense of power. This power is ALL YOURS, baby, and you get to use it to make the biggest of dreams come true!

When I learn something, I cannot unlearn it. When I know something I cannot pretend that I do not. It is so apparent to me that we stop ourselves from greatness all the time because we are conditioned to strive for normal so we fit in. I don't want to be normal. I want to shine in all the power of my special gifts and be totally in line from my head down and my heart out. It is this alignment that creates an effortless life. Please feel free to join me!

Recently, and purely by accident, I spent some time in the St James Market in Victoria. I had time to kill and happened to park my car in the same lot as the market so I wandered over. I loved the atmosphere – live music, meandering people, stalls filled with entrepreneurs selling the items they had created with passion. I strolled through and made a few purchases and connections. When I decided it was time for a coffee, the tables near the music were all partially full. I saw a women sitting alone and asked if I could join her. I sat down and we began chatting. In time, a few of her friends joined us. Have you ever had a moment or a conversation where suddenly you realize you are in a time and place and it doesn't feel accidental at all? I left that market thinking about the limits I put upon myself to live within the constraints of what is deemed normal. I want to play near the edges, tumble over them and stretch myself to new dimensions. While I am always pushing myself to stretch, this day at the market enlightened me in new ways and made me more aware, yet again, of things I could change. When you begin this journey, you must realize that you will likely never arrive at THE destination because your destination changes as you grow. If you happen to arrive, you will not stay long!

Chapter 6:
CREATING SPACE BY LETTING GO

When I first started my journey from WTF to OMG, I know I had stopped dreaming about things I wanted to have in my life. I think it became a luxury I decided I couldn't afford as an adult, a mother, and a grown-up. It wasn't really practical. My time was better spent doing one more load of laundry or trying to catch up with my work. Even if I had sat still long enough to create an image of this life I wanted for myself, I am not sure I was capable then. You can't be that wrecked and approach dreaming with any sense of sincerity, because it all seems so far away. All I was dreaming about was a beach, a very strong umbrella drink, and silence.

The status quo, as I had partly established it, had no space for me to create the life I wanted for myself, or my family. There was no joy there. I knew if I stayed in that place, there was NO hope of something different for any of us. No hope there. None. Zippo. Nada.

It was time to create space. Purge. De-clutter. Streamline. It was during this phase, I realized how much negative energy stuff could hold. I began to realize that simplicity is bliss. I began to see simplicity decreased the stress, made things more clear, and helped me stay focused.

Liberation in Letting Go

With a new sense of clarity about what you want from your life, it will suddenly become easier to let go of the stuff that doesn't help you get there. It is considerably harder to let go of things if you do not know where you are headed. Things can appear to serve as safety nets. But, have you ever considered that by holding on to things you have placed the safety net **above** your head instead of below your feet? Is it possible that your well-intentioned safety net is not keeping you from falling but keeping you from taking flight? Holy shit Batman! Now that's a huge "aha" and I think I felt the earth move.

Essentially, you can hang onto a bunch of things "just in case" this or that doesn't work out. But in all reality, holding onto stuff, things, and people that serve an intention long passed, is a nice way of telling yourself, "Hey Loser, you are going to fail at this and when you do, we will be here to soften the landing. If you let go and you fail, you will have nothing. Yes, that is right. NOTHING. Better hang on to us. WE don't believe in your success anymore than you do." (AH! See how fear plays into the process of letting go so you can move on? Tricky bitch!)

In case you didn't notice, there is a very strong relationship between the ability to let go of things and fear of all the things that can happen if you do. But, I urge you to consider how easier it is to fly when you do not have to carry things that drain you of your energy, focus, and brilliance.

Make Letting Go Symbolic

After my dad's accident and the newly considered decision to actually go to Ironman, I had a sixteen-hour drive ahead of me and plenty of time to think about my life. The WTF Moment, the changes I had made to my life and to my overall wellness, and here I was preparing to complete in an Ironman Distance Triathlon. Holy crap! The magnitude of the changes silenced me for a while. I had many things to celebrate and still, I knew I had some unresolved "issues" holding me back. Dad's recent accident had really kicked things up a notch.

ONE LIFE. We only get one. Was I doing the best I could with mine?

So many things were swirling inside my head and heart. Things I thought I had dealt with started surfacing because of the realization that my father's time on earth almost came to an end in a blink of an eye. I was suddenly more aware of the fragility of life than I had ever been. I promised myself that day that I would let go of all these things that I was still carrying with me. Loss, divorce, failure, sadness, anger, regret, guilt ... it all had to go.

The Ironman bike course is a challenging one, known for Richter's Pass and the rollers (each of the rollers representing a climb on the course). I decided that at the top of each climb, I was going to make a verbal statement about something I had been carrying with me and then I was going to leave it on the mountain. I was going to let it go. I was going to stop carrying all this "stuff" with me so I could lighten my load. I imagined (visualized) feeling lighter after cresting each climb, dropping the baggage, and carrying on.

I needed to let go of the failures I felt as a result of my divorce because my divorce had been for the best even though it was a hard decision. It was also approached with only good intentions and I needed to now appreciate the gifts the marriage gave me: two great kids, a few awesome lessons, some joy, some sorrow, and new perspectives about relationships. Richter got this one because it was the heaviest. The rollers that followed got the rest. I needed to deal with the loss of my grandparents. It's hard to explain that one, but I had some unresolved thinking. I resolved it and what I couldn't, I let go. Sadness, anger, regret, life balance, guilt ... I left it all on the mountain. I loved the symbolic nature of my approach too.

I had finally learned how much power there is in letting go if you truly let go. I had finally realized letting go doesn't mean you never cared, or that an event or person never mattered. I realized you could have the lesson without the suffering. I had finally learned that letting go frees you to move out of places that you have outgrown.

Toxic People

Letting go of stuff and emotions is one thing, but letting go of toxic people is another thing entirely. However, people can be extremely toxic to your progress and if they can't be managed in a manner that ensures they do no harm, they must be released. It's that simple. There are many variations of the toxic person: but the common attribute they share is that their presence in your life actually keeps you from achieving what you desire. You could have a little Miss Negativity, or Miss Passive Aggressive, or Mr. Bossy Pants in your life. You could have Chronic Liar, Needy Nelda, Back Stabber Sue, or Copy Cat Clyde messing with all the good you try to do!

The irony is that some toxic people can be so wrapped up in you and your success that they never pay any attention to their own amazing gifts. They want what you have, or they are jealous of it, or they do not understand it. They see your authenticity, your effortlessness, and how powerful you have become by getting clear about what you want and they want to feel that way too. It is almost like they panic. They have some warped idea that if they are just like you, they will get it all, too, but they can never be you.

We both know, they need to focus on themselves and that the answer to their own power, authenticity, and success is about self-discovery not mimicking others. But until they get that they hang around like an irritating fly, always in your business, trying to see what you are doing, and offering to help but causing stress instead. Until they understand that YOU do not have THEIR answers, and that they will not have access to their own power until they learn how to value their own gifts, they remain soured, obnoxious, and toxic to your success if you allow them to be too close.

I have noticed that many toxic people often move on without you having to push them away when your focus is directed at what you want and you stop engaging in their dramatic behaviors. You change the rules of the game and shift the dynamics.

But not all of them vanish so easily. I am reminded of a particular person who was brilliant in her own right. Smart and creative, she had endless successes under her belt. But she was always watching other people and wanted to know what other people were saying and doing. Her insecurities were glaringly apparent to me, and many others, and it always seemed like she did not have an appreciation for her own gifts. She couldn't look at her skill set and see what others could. She could find no value in her own unique abilities. She was always looking over the fence wanting to be like someone else. She was paranoid people were talking about her. She was in such a tither about other people and what they were doing that she was ineffective and annoying. She was so broken and disconnected from her own skills and strengths and so busy trying to be like everyone else that she totally discounted her own strengths and power.

Had she took the time to learn a little bit about herself and settle into her strengths she would have multiplied her effectiveness ten fold and she would become a source of inspiration for others. She needed to stop trying to be like everyone else and learn to love who she was. Despite her talents, I stopped associating with her because her energy caused me stress and diverted my focus from what mattered to me. She wasn't a bad person, nor was she unlikable but her vibe was poison to what I was trying to establish.

We are all a force to be reckoned with when we find our connection to our purpose.
Have you found yours?

Since Ironman 2008, I have refined my ability to identify and let go of more and more things that hinder my progress. I attached the process of letting go to the intentions I have set out for myself and it has made letting go effortless. I invite you to do the same by following the activity below.

SWIFTKICK TIP: Clear the Decks

If simplicity is bliss, I encourage you to look at your life with true honesty and see where you can simplify. Can you tell the difference between a want and a need? Do you really need the new shoes or do you want them? I am not saying you cannot have the shoes, but you must to be aware of what your possession of them serves. Do you buy things to fill the voids in your life? Do you feed yourself with stuff in an effort to find happiness? When you can differentiate a need from a want and then confront the wants head on, you can discover some interesting things about yourself.

In the chapter, *What Do You Really Want?* my goal was to move you into a place where you could begin to clarify your thinking. When you are clear about what you want, you can purge your life of the clutter with such an increased ease, that you will wonder why it was hard to let go of anything in the first place.

If you have done the work in the previous chapter, I want you to write down one of your intentions in the box. If not, return here when you have done the work.

We will try this on your physical environment first. With your intention top of mind, walk around your home. Pick up an item that you see, and just ask, "Does this item serve my intention? Will this item help me get where I want to be or does it hold me back?" If the item is something that will help you (say it's a pair of brand new running shoes and your intention is to focus on your fitness) then you know it serves your intentions. The shoes can stay. Go ahead and try it right now. I will wait. No, really go ahead! You have to see how easy this is when you have your intention connected to the process of letting go!

Now let's say you pick up an older pair of shoes with no support left in them. Ask yourself again, "Does this serve my intention?" Given they are old and could lead to injury if you run long distances without proper support, you know they do not serve your intention. In fact, they could serve as an obstacle if you use them and get injured because of lack of support. They can go.

If you picked up an item that doesn't help or hinder your intentions, you can always ask yourself if you need it, or if it is just a form of clutter that requires energy for you to deal with it on a daily basis. Let's say you have picked up a vase your ex-husband gave you. It's pretty and you love the gold-embossed vase and the time in your life it represents but every time you look at the vase it takes you to a place that reminds you of loss, sadness, or anger. It certainly isn't serving a purpose of bringing you joy and it could be a subconscious energy drain. Does it serve you to be visiting these exhausting emotional places? No, it does not. So ... you say, "Pretty little vase, enjoy your new home. You served me once, but now I am a different person heading somewhere else. I need to let you go."

Letting go of old clothes, old feelings, old furniture, and old things is liberating. It's energizing. Things in our environment can trigger unresolved feelings and the first step in getting rid of the nonproductive emotions is to get rid of the things we have attached these emotions to. It's like cracking open a can of soda water, the pressure is released and ahhhh, you feel so much better. You create a more simple, streamlined life that DOES serve your intentions. If everything in your life and your world was there on purpose and it supported and served your intentions, think of the power that environment would release for your use as you move forward into your OMG Life!

If you are feeling overwhelmed and do not think you have the energy to do this task alone, invite your best friends over and open a few bottles of wine. Not only will they be able to keep you on task, they will constantly remind you of how awesome you are, support you when you need it, and girlfriends are PRO at using humor to offset some of the anxiety you may feel about letting go and moving on. Feels like a win-win to me!

Clear the deck or you will stay stuck. It is that simple. If you save your fat pants, you are saying you need them for when you fail....again. If you keep your toxic relationships, when you begin to move into a brighter future, they will drag you back down.

Off you go now! Walk around your house and pick up five items. Simply ask yourself, "Does this serve my intentions?" If it does, keep it and move on. If it doesn't, move it to the back door and take it to charity in the morning. The shift you will experience is immediate. Make sure you do this activity so you can experience it. I ended up having to call a local dumping company once I caught on to how powerful this strategy was and it felt incredible!

Chapter 7:
DON'T LIKE IT? MOVE TOWARDS WHAT YOU PREFER!

It's time to become fully aware of the choices you make every single day. Equally important is that you must become aware of the choices you are NOT making for yourself. A million things can happen in a day that just seem to "happen automatically" because someone else decides for you. Sorry, no more meandering along. It is time to become alert. Conscious. Alive.

Every single choice you make (or do not make) takes you in a certain direction. You are going to start making choices that take you in the direction YOU WANT TO GO. If you do not know exactly where you want to go, then often other people decide where you are going to go because it doesn't much matter to you. Choices lead to actions. We want you moving away from what you do not want and moving towards what you desire from the bottom of your beautiful, loving heart.

We want your choices to be conscious and we want them to move you away from "crazy town" and towards bliss, away from drama and towards fun, freedom, and joy. Even if you do not know exactly what you want at this point, it is very likely you know what you do not want. So if you are not entirely clear yet, make sure you make choices that move you away from the things you **know** you do not want. And pay attention to that gut! Feelings are fabulously intelligent.

A quick illustration: Let's say that you are in a social situation, perhaps in an establishment with some girlfriends for a night out. Your party is having a great time when "creepy guy" enters the picture. You and your friends, for the most part are single, but you know immediately that "creepy guy" is not for any of you. He is well on his way to being intoxicated, and he is draping himself over you and your friends like a sly tomcat. Your party tries to be gracious and polite at first, telling him that none of you are interested, but thanks. He persists.

Instead of you all crawling into his lap and running your fingers through his hair, your party MOVES TOWARDS an alternative arrangement and away from what isn't working. You all decide to switch tables to a place further back in the establishment and let "creepy guy" drink himself into a hangover alone. It's an easy decision because even though you do not know for sure what you DO want in a partner, you are very clear about what you DO NOT want. Easy-peasy.

You end up seated next to a table of interesting looking men, some polished and some a little more rough around the edges. They give off a totally different vibe. It's like a single girl's dream variety pack. Conversation at your table quickly switches over to discussing the love-lies at the table next to you. Eyelashes flutter and eye contact is made.

Before you know it, tables have been pulled together and new friends made. While you are not sure there is anyone specifically at the new table that you feel an attraction to, the vibe is friendly and fun. You moved away from what you knew you didn't want and towards an alternative and ended up having a great time that evening. Turns out, Ed, who was seated at the table you joined, had a good friend who joined them later and the two of you hit it off right away. Life is funny like that. Moving away from what doesn't serve you often leads you to opportunities three deep that do. It puts you in a different place energetically. Yeah, baby, are you starting to sense the power of OMG creeping up on you?

SWIFTKICK TIP: Moving Away/ Moving Towards
Take a minute and think about three things you know for certain you do not want to be a part of your life. This can include people, jobs, activities, and other elements like junk food, toxic relationships, and the like.

Write down your three items and beside each one, write, in detail, what moving away from the item would look like.

For example:

1. Car payments: Secure secondary work to finally pay off car, or investigate public transport and determine if it is a feasible option for lifestyle. If so, sell car.
2. Toxic friends: Avoid the group that hangs out at "The Bar" by scheduling gym dates and healthy living activities on Friday evenings.
3. Poor eating habits: Grocery shop on Sunday and do meal prep so good food is on hand. Do not bring any junk into the house.

Ok, your turn! Make your list and write out in detail what moving away from each item on YOUR list would look like. Tweet me your list!

Then, make these new behaviors actionable and schedule the new behaviors into your planner. Ready, set, go!

Creating a stopping list and identifying what things you need to move away from is a simple, yet powerful, way to create some space in your life quickly. You can make rapid progress with these tips so get your butt in gear!

Chapter 8:
FEAR - YOU CAN'T BE A SCAREDY CAT

"We invent what we love, and what we fear." - John Irving

Fear is a funny thing. I try to do something on purpose that scares me as often as I can, solely for the purpose of reminding myself how great it feels to overcome a fear. I love being intimate with that sense of freedom. It's energizing. Fear isn't anything other than a bunch of "things" we conjure up in our minds to create an idea of how things will play out. Fear projects us into the future, removes us from the now, and creeps through our brains making us ask a handful of "what if" questions that introduce anxiety and panic. Fear isn't even real. It isn't an apple you can take out of your pocket and bite into. It hasn't happened. When I am fearful, it is my imagination writing how a certain story will end. I often forget I have the power at any time to change the way the story goes and so do you.

Fear loves your baggage, too, so if there is any possible way for fear to grab hold of negative past experiences and bring them along into the imagined future, it will. (My first marriage didn't work out so I fear this one won't either.) Fear will remind you what happened last time, so you better expect it to happen again. If something didn't turn out well for you in the past, and you develop a belief system based on that experience, fear is right there to claim some energy from that negative experience so it can grow and flourish before you get a chance to think it through and toss it into a headlock.

What The Zipper Taught Me

When I was in about grade seven, the little fair that came to the local mall was a highlight for a few of my "prime" middle school years. My girlfriends and I would put on our Fancy Ass Jeans, sausage curl our hair, layer on the blue eye shadow, and off we would go. My sister always rode the Zipper. I always wanted to but I was so scared of that ride and I have no idea where the fear came from. It didn't matter that she loved it and she rode it over and over again. It didn't even matter that she looked like she was having the time of her life. My fear of that ride and what would happen to me on it was so enormous that common sense couldn't infiltrate it.

I would spend an evening at the fair, watching people get on and off the Zipper. Each time I had a chance to get in line, I backed out. For about three years, I wasted an entire evening of my life doing that, on the brink of tears because I was so frustrated with myself. I brewed for days afterwards, angry that I couldn't just belly up and get on the ride. This mattered to me in a way no one seemed to understand. I am now forty-two and I can remember vividly what it felt like to be that afraid, and to be that angry with myself for letting fear take away an opportunity. When my anger surpassed my fear, I promised myself that, no matter what, the following summer I would get on that ride.

"Inaction breeds doubt and fear. Action breeds confidence and courage. If you want to conquer fear, do not sit home and think about it. Go out and get busy." - Dale Carnegie

Guess what? I didn't die.

It wasn't even that scary. Life went on and I never wasted my energy thinking about that ride again. But I have used this experience time and time again to remind myself how free I felt to finally conquer that fear. The longer I avoided it, the stronger it became. It wasn't even rational! That was just one ride at the annual fair, imagine what fear can do to your life if you let it grow and take control.

"You gain strength, courage and confidence by every experience in which you really stop to look fear in the face. You must do the thing you think you cannot do." – Eleanor Roosevelt

Re-Focus a Fear

This past year, I went to Mexico with my boyfriend. I told Jason I needed to do something that scared me on our trip, after all I was long overdue. Zip-lining was on the fear list. Surfing was, too. (I am afraid of all aquatic life despite having temporarily overcome it to finish two 3.8 kilometer open water swim legs in Lake Okanagan. You know, where the Ogopogo lives? Which by the way means "lake demon").

I am truly afraid of things in the water. Irrational? Absolutely. (Well, sort of because there are things in the water that CAN kill you). I am a strong swimmer but a weed tangled in my feet can send me into a total meltdown. It is totally irrational. Remember, I never claimed I was perfect, and I do still have some fears to face but the main thing is – don't let yourself become frozen with fear, push through it.

"There is no terror in the bang, only in the anticipation of it." - Alfred Hitchcock

We found a zip-line tour nearby and booked an expedition. I remember hanging off the zip-line waiting to go, and I couldn't breathe. The more I thought about the fact I couldn't breathe, the more I couldn't breathe. The lovely guide reminded me I was not scared of heights, just scared of falling. He told me I wouldn't fall, as he pointed to the TWO safety cables. I focused on his lips as he spoke. I could feel my heart in my chest, my breath being squeezed out of my lungs, but I focused on his lips. I watched them move. I wondered if he had a little shot of filler in the top one. I wondered if he knew I was using his lips as a distraction. Did he feel dirty? Ha! I listened to how quiet it was around me and reminded myself how blessed I was to be here to experience this with someone who was special to me (my boyfriend, not the guide).

I stopped focusing on the fear I had and started focusing on other things. It took a few minutes before I interrupted my fear cycle. I then reminded myself I wouldn't fall and even if I did, I wouldn't likely remember it. Either way, I was going to push off the cliff and jump into my fear. I leaned in hard and my feet left the earth. My squeals filled the valley and I was flying.

Can't Focus on Two Things

When you fear something, best to get yourself something other than that fear to focus on, even if it is a random item like a tour guide's lips. Why? Simply put, it is pretty hard to focus on two things at once, especially if they are asking you to feel two different emotions or require two very different things of you (gratitude versus fear). It is kind of that "rub your tummy pat your head" trick that I could never do. If I focused on patting my head I was a good patter. If I focused on rubbing my belly, the patting went to hell in a hand basket. Fast.

True focus can only go to one thing at one time, pick your poison, baby, because if you do not, fear has a way of picking it for you. And that just sucks.

I was surfing the Web one day and I came across Matthew Child's TED Talk, "Hang in there! 9 life lessons from rock climbing." (http://blog.ted.com/2009/04/17/hang_in_there_9/)

Matthew struck a chord with me when he explained, "fear really sucks because you are not focusing on what you are *doing* but instead you are focusing on the *consequences of failing* at what you are doing." (Um, yeah, like I am going to fall from the zip-line cable.)

Understanding the role that focus plays in the state of fear really hit home because it makes sense to me on a personal level. When I am swimming in open water for a triathlon, I am focused entirely on that swim and I have no fear. (Between you and me, I think my odds of survival go up when there are more possible victims in the water with me.) If I am trying to do an open water training swim and I am not really that focused on the workout, I have energy to give to a fear and I feed it by focusing on it. The more I feed it, the more panic-stricken I become. Focus instead on what you want, not the fear. Feed the dream. It's mind over matter.

Common Fears That Keep You Stuck

Fear can keep you stuck but you can move through it, over it, or around it if you take back some control by breaking fear down. Common fears that keep people stuck include fear of embarrassment or looking bad, abandonment, being hurt, failure, and a big one is fear that if people get to know the "real you" they will no longer like you (which makes the entire be real chapter even more important). A variation of that is a fear that once you discover who you are as you move towards fulfilling your purpose, people you care about will dislike the "real" you, will complain that you have changed, that things are not the same and hold you responsible for changing a relationship that was once "so good" (in their books, not necessarily yours).

You can also fear being powerful. You can fear standing out. You can fear not being good enough, fast enough, tall enough, thin enough, rich enough, funny enough or smart enough. Do you ever feel like you are not enough?

Anyone who has seen a relationship end might be left asking, "Why wasn't I enough?" I urge you to consider that you were enough, you have always been enough, and perhaps your ex-partner just needed something different, not something more or something better. Ever seen two amazing people struggle to make a relationship work? Just because they were both amazing, doesn't mean they were meant to be.

Every one of us is enough just as we are and we become more powerful as we learn how to be true to our own needs. We dilute ourselves when we do not follow our purpose. You have to have faith in yourself to take risks and embrace fear, and if you fail, that failure might be releasing you from one thing to move you closer to something else that is magnitudes of bliss beyond what you were originally trying to achieve. Fear can fuel you or it can burn you. Again, the choice is yours.

Fear, in any form, keeps you perched on the mountain of life's zip-lining adventures, hanging there, frozen. It is up to you take back control and put that fear into is place! **What we focus on expands**. Knowing this, if you focus on a fear, you make it bigger and more powerful. Focusing on your fears can become a habitual way of thinking (seriously, with neural pathways that encourage more and more of it) and that kind of thinking isn't going to take you where you want to go.

Fear is an illusion. Your body's reaction to what you are thinking brings about the feelings we associate with fear. These feelings encourage you to worry about things that have not yet happened in a time and place that has yet to arrive. Fear is also often based on assumptions that the event you fear will give birth to the "worst-ever possible" scenarios. The man you fancy won't just hate you, he will scream at the top of his lungs what a disgusting person you are and post it all over Facebook to boot! You won't just screw up that interview, the interviewer will stop mid sentence and ask, "Who the hell are you to come in here and waste my time pretending you are actually qualified to do this job?" And that speech you were asked to give at your best friends wedding? Surely you realize that you will stand up there, break out in speaker's rash, crash with all your jokes, and vomit down the front of your gown only to be tagged in a video of it all posted on a video-sharing website. Sometimes our fear is a tad bit over dramatized.

When we stand up to face a fear that has really had an oppressive impact on us (and often for a long period of time), it is usually a WTF Moment that triggers the flight or fight response. We feel cornered like a wild animal, pushed deeply into the dark, and we finally feel like we can't stay there afraid anymore. Essentially, we reach our breaking point.

We come out swinging with one purpose only and that is to win. That's why WTF Moments often provide you with the energy you need to tackle things you thought you couldn't previously. We shift focus to what we can control, not fear. And, it's the things you CAN control that take you where you need to go! You know what that means, buttercup? Yes, once again, it is up to you!

SWIFTKICK TIP: Give Fear The Boot

Fear is a response to what doesn't currently exist for sure, yet. Fear is the anticipation of what might happen. That anticipation can be more detrimental to your well-being than the actual event you fear. Fear sucks the energy out of your tank faster than a hole in a boat. Fear is fed by our decision to feed it. So stop it! Stop feeding your fears. Feed your dreams instead. Change your thoughts and your feelings will follow.

Here is a commonly used five-step process that can help you to "deflate a fear" and regain a sense of power over how you feel about a situation.

1. Name your fear – don't just say I am scared about this or that. Be specific. You have to be specific because you need to know exactly what to challenge. "I am scared that if I get divorced, I will be left trying to support these two kids alone and I do not have the means to do so." Or, "I am scared I will go to this interview and be humiliated and no one will take me seriously."

2. Ask yourself, what is the WORST thing that could happen if you forged ahead and made your move (in this case, got divorced or went to that interview). "I would be extremely poor and my life would be very hard." "I would crash and burn under pressure in the interview."

3. Ask questions that force you to answer them to remove assumptions. "Would your husband really turn his back on the obligation to the kids?" Yes? OK, then that is the scenario you use moving forward. You wouldn't be able to depend on him financially or emotionally. Is this going to kill you? How can you plan for this?

   Or, "Would your husband really turn his back on the obligation to the kids?" No. I am just pissed at him right now and do not like how he is behaving. I think he would help a bit but I am uncertain what that looks like." Ok, so use this scenario to plan moving forward. With some help from him, where does that leave you? Be specific. Research child support laws in your place of residence. Examine options.

   Or, what about that interview? Do you really think you are going to blow this interview and be humiliated? If not, stop feeding yourself all that negativity. Use visualization tactics in the next section to practice the perfect kickass interview. If you are uncertain, how can you best prepare for it? If you fail, what can you learn so the next interview is better? Use each interview as a way to refine your skills.

4. Ask the hard questions. Get the information you need to make informed decisions. Do NOT sit there fretting, start gathering facts – gather as many as you can because they are WAY less scary than assumptions!

5. If my greatest fear came true in this scenario, what would it take for me to recover from it? Is it possible some opportunities I cannot see right now might appear and take me in directions I have never thought of before? (This one is a chewy question because you have no idea what is out there for you and if you change your thinking, you become open to things you do not see right now.)

Think about your original fear, have you deflated it a little bit? Can you sense that fear losing some of its power because you are not wasting valuable energy worrying about "what ifs"? Can you feel the slight shifts because you have been more specific about what exactly it is you fear and then you have called it out and challenged assumptions? Keep at it and you can reduce these fears that have kept you stuck and soon you will be able to step over them with ease!

Chapter 9:
DECISIONS DETERMINE DIRECTION

I understand that many of us know already what the right decision may be for our various situations. And, we'd do almost anything possible to stuff that realization into deep, dark hiding places so we can ignore it! We have the beautiful gift of intuition but we fail to honor it. We know the answer but we still stay stuck because of our fears. Now that we have addressed the power of fear and given you some tactics for decreasing it, you need to examine your fears, shrink them and get ready to make some choices. Also, if you understand the concept that what you focus on expands, you can see why actually deciding something and then focusing on that decision can begin to expand your life in a new way and pull your feet out of the quicksand.

When we hang around in a holding pattern, tossing around all the things we could, should, or ought to do but we fall short of actually making a decision, we cheat ourselves of the energy that is actually released when we make a decision. As soon as you make a decision, let's say to end a relationship, go back to school, or quit a job, you immediately know what the next step is. If you are ending a relationship, you may need a new place to live. If you are going back to school, you need to find out how you sign up and if you are quitting your job you can start looking forward to other opportunities. But, if you remain in limbo just tossing the ideas around and stop short of deciding, you never look past where you are right now. You don't get to decide which road you are going to take when you approach the fork in the road! You miss all the opportunities the universe is trying to provide you because you are indecisive. You constantly miss the boat and the opportunities.

Many of us have a fear of making the wrong decision. But the bottom line is that NOT making a decision is actually making one. Deciding not to take action is actively choosing the status quo. You are deciding to stay exactly where you are! S.T.U.C.K. Blah!

And you know what? Think through how making the wrong decision and moving out of where you are, even if it is not towards your ideal place, is better than staying where you currently are. What if you learn a valuable lesson because of a bad decision and the opportunity to learn that lesson is the ONE lesson that changes everything for you. Bad decisions can be huge learning opportunities and they can release you from being stuck and they can help you face your fears.

A quick illustration: A few years back I was feeling like my job was not as satisfying for me as it had been so I was looking at going back to school. But, I had a great job in terms of flexibility and in many ways it felt better to me than some of the other options out there. I was being honest with myself and I knew I was losing my zest for what I was doing. I was hesitant to make the decision final because I was scared that upon my return from leave, I would be assigned a less-desirable position. But, I also thought that no matter what, I would learn something and my new post could be awesome. I made the decision to go back to school.

I was excited about the schooling and looking forward to the change. What I could never have foreseen was that my daughter would begin having absent seizures by November and grand mal seizures by December of the year I was on educational leave. I had my year of study and travel planned and nowhere in that plan did I write "child gets sick!"

However, being on leave that year instead of at my prior job turned out to be an incredible blessing. I was able to work on my studies even when she was sick (if I wasn't too exhausted) and I was able to rearrange my days around surprise seizures, emergency room visits, and doctor appointments. Making that decision to return to school put me in a place where I could manage her illness way more effectively and still work towards my own goals. It was an incredibly productive year. There is no doubt in my mind that I would have been unable to work my previous job that year. My daughter wasn't even attending school for about four months. We had a tutor from the hospital coming to try to keep her up on her studies, and she required a high level of supervision!

Even more amazing to me was that as the year's leave started coming to a close and I was looking ahead to the next year, I was getting increasingly more and more anxious about leaving my daughter alone before school hours in the house, and I was concerned about her walking in the frigid winter temperatures "just in case" something happened. She was on medications but she was far from stable. Job postings were coming up often and I was unsure what I should apply for given all these things happening on the home front. So, I decided to ask for help. I called a superintendent and explained my situation to see if he could offer some suggestions, because I needed to work.

I wondered how I would explain my anxiety to the lucky person who got my call but the universe put me in good hands. I started the conversation explaining that my daughter was diagnosed with epilepsy and we were still trying to get her stable and I began to discuss my anxiety about not being there for her when I broke down crying. Yep, I felt like an unprofessional loser and I didn't think anyone would understand what I was going through when the person on the other end said, "I totally understand what you are going through, both my wife and my son have epilepsy. Let's just talk through some of this."

BIG. HUGE. DEEP. BREATH. I didn't have to explain how things could be fine and then not fine three seconds later. I didn't have to explain how the meds were making her sleepy and lethargic. I didn't have to explain how I was scared for her safety. As a parent, he knew first hand what I was facing.

So looking back now on the decision I made to go back to school, I would have decided to do that FOR SURE had I known what was in store for me. And yes, I ended up in a totally outstanding school, with EXTREMELY supportive staff and administrators as I navigated the first year back to work. It couldn't have worked out any better had I planned it. I also feel strongly that had it not worked out this way, something would have because I believe that is the way it all works!

So besides fear holding you back from making decisions, we some-times have patterns of decision-making that keep us dodging the final choice. What decisions might you avoid making consistently and why might that be? For example, when I was going through my divorce I didn't want to make any financial decisions because I felt so uncertain. I would make all other kinds of decisions, no problem, but I stumbled when it came to financial ones. Then one day it dawned on me that I needed to be making these decisions or one day I would wake up and my inaction would have me poorly prepared for retirement. That scared me even more than making a wrong choice now because I knew I would still have time to correct a mistake I might make now.

I also received some great advice about making decisions that move you towards your dreams. It makes things much easier and changes the way you think and feel. Are you ready?

Make decisions based on who you want to be, not who you currently are!
So what does that mean? It means if you want to be a seriously kickass businesswoman, make the decisions she would make. If you want to train for and complete a marathon, make the decisions a marathoner would make. It makes perfect sense that by doing so, over time you end up exactly where you want to be!

A discussion about your decisions would not be complete without a nod to the fear that your decisions will disappoint others. And yes, they might do just that but you cannot let the disappointment that others feel about your choices influence what you decide. Free yourself from that fear by reminding yourself that you are responsible for your own happiness and everyone else is responsible for his or her own happiness. You cannot control how people choose to react to what you decide to do; you can only control your own choices and behaviors. Yes, it is really that simple, if you believe you deserve to be happy!

The hard truth is that you NEED to learn to make decisions. If not making decision is keeping you trapped, you have nothing to lose by actually being active in the process and you have enormous momentum to gain. When you decide what you are going to do, you are released from the grips of limbo and free to begin creating a plan that will get you where you want to be!

SWIFTKICK TIP: Coin Flip and Your Body Truth
Having a hard time making a decision? Here is one piece of advice that I received from a friend that has proven to be bang on.

Flip a coin.

Yep, flip a coin. And pay close attention to your body's reactions or "body truth." Use this approach to access your intuition, if your mind is trying to be a big, fat bully. In general, if you are about to make a bad decision you will likely feel your body contracting in some way. It is pulling in to protect itself. If you are about to make a good decision, you will feel yourself expand. You will be excited, have butterflies, and a renewed sense of energy. Feeling your body contract or expand can be very subtle. But the flipping of a coin forces your focus to a moment when you see how the flip turned out. If you immediately wished it was the other way, you have an answer about how you truly feel. If you are disappointed with the outcome, then you know that is the wrong decision to make. This is really useful if you have been bashing you head into a wall analyzing your issues until your brain is mush.

A client was tossing around the question, "Do I want to stay in my current relationship and try to make it work even though the other person had been unfaithful?" This client had analyzed the options to death and was tied to the relationship with a very heavy sense of duty. Nothing seemed any more clear despite the analyzing. There were complicated issues like kids, assets, and unrealized dreams. Deep down, there were doubts about having settled earlier in life because it seemed like marriage was the next responsible step to take. I gave these instructions.

Ask yourself your question. "Do I want to try to stay in this relationship and make it work even though they have been unfaithful to me?

Pick heads for YES and pick tails for NO.

Flip the coin. Pay close attention to how you feel the immediate moment you hear the answer to the flip. It landed on heads (which meant YES she should stay and work it out). She felt disappointed. Sad. She didn't want to stay.

I asked her to consider how NO felt. It felt scary and uncertain but better than YES. She has since moved on into a new life and feels like she made the best choice and is happy with how her new life is coming together.

If you have a tough decision hanging over your head that you have beat the crap out of, try this simple strategy and see what happens. Pay close attention to your body's reaction.

Chapter 10:
HOW TO GET SATISF-ACTION

Now that you have learned why making decisions or not making them, impacts your life we need to talk a little bit about all the wonderful actionable steps that can follow the bliss of making a decision. First off, facing any fears to make a decision and begin acting gives you confidence and that is never a bad thing. Once you have made a decision you know what direction you are heading. Everything becomes increasingly clear when you have made a decision because all the other options fall away and you can focus on what actions you need to do complete to make all things fall together. Easy, right? Well, not always.

Knowing It and Doing It
If I have made the decision to get fit and healthy, I know the actions I must take in order to make this happen. Most people do. However, knowing what needs to be done and actually DOING what needs to be done are two very different things. It is all about taking action!

You may have great ideas about who you want to be but unless you start doing something about it, you are just a dreamer. What are you waiting for? If you start now, you are on your way. If you wait a year, you have an extra year of bad habits and their consequences to undo. The quickest way to build momentum is to start ACTING on what you have decided.

One of the most effective strategies I have found for creating an action plan is to grab my planner and start scheduling in things that I need to DO in order to move towards my goal. I can work from where I am towards the end goal or I can work from the end goal backwards, but the most important thing is that once I write the actions into my planner, they are no longer optional. The planner becomes my action plan. I consider the actions promises I make to myself, and I am a girl of my word!

SWIFTKICK TIP: Protect Your Work

You do all this work and start taking action. You make changes no one ever thought YOU were capable of and you ride off into the sunset as the credits roll. Not so fast. You have done all this work but you can not simply go back to just existing or you will end up exactly where you were and you will need to get all scrappy again to get back here. Pay close attention here so that all of your hard work doesn't go to waste!

You have read some heavy thoughts and you have done serious work to dig through your less pleasant "stuff" to start creating a life you love. Now you need to protect the work you have done because if you do not protect it then you risk ending up back where you started. Put strategies and scripts in place to protect all your progress and to prevent new stresses from coming into your life and filling the space you just cleared. I think about what happens when kids start building sand castles on the beach: if they do not build a protective gate, the ocean washes up and tears down all the progress they have made.

For example, I love to help people. Because of my experience with Ironman and various fitness related activities, people always ask me for free fitness advice. They ask me to basically create a meal plan and a work out plan on the fly – in line at the grocery store. I give them as much help as I can but I also have put free advice on my website so I can direct people to it and not have to spend precious time repeating the basics over and over again. One of my "gates" to protect my precious time that I fought hard to reclaim is to ask them, "What exactly are you looking for? If you need a few tips, I have some free downloads on my website that may be of help to you but if you are needing to speak to me personally about your situation, please feel free to book an appointment with me at a time that works for you. My fee is $/hour." This allows me to be as helpful as I can, but it also protects my time that I need to earn a living and it prevents me from being taken advantage of by people who may not understand that I do this for a living.

Another gate might be a rule you implement to avoid having a crash landing or falling off the fitness wagon (if you have a fitness-related goal). Let's say you have learned that hanging out with your work buddies at the local pub on Friday evenings leads to over consumption of alcohol and unhealthy food choices, you might put a rule in place that allows you to take part in the "Friday Night Shenanigans" once every eight weeks. You follow the rule and you stay on the wagon!

Another example might be that you find Monday mornings are always stressful for you running around with kids and lunches and last minute forms that need to be signed, so you decide to place a gate to prevent this. You make Sunday evenings the time for a quick family meeting about what is coming up for the week. The kids make lists and put them on their bedroom doors, you delegate responsibility where it belongs, you discuss and plan meals, and you go through their forms and sign them all and tuck them back into their bags. When Monday morning rolls around there are no big surprises, and no additional stress. You have protected the work you have done to date by making sure that everyone is responsible for himself or herself. You have not started to take over responsibilities that do not belong to you because you are in Monday-morning panic mode.

My golden rule is this: Do NOT put yourself into a situation that you know (based on previous experience) is going to threaten the work you have already done and the progress you have already made UNLESS you have a strategy or script to get yourself quickly out of the situation if need be. You got my drift, sister? This is about having your OWN back!

PART 4:
Getting What You Want

The quality of your self-care forms the foundation that you are going to build the rest of your life upon. Just like any building with a faulty foundation, if your self-care is poor or non-existent, the life you build on it can only handle so much stress before it crumples like a house of cards.

Look at you rock your way through this book! I am so proud of you! Grab another drink if you need one but only if your comprehension isn't going to be impaired. We are in the home stretch, darling, and I need to make sure you are paying attention! I am almost ready to let you whip up a shitload of OMG!

We have covered the big problems (your WTF life) and looked at the power behind the big solution (mindset shift) and discussed methods of implementing a plan but there are a few little secrets left to share.

I need to discuss with you the importance of building a strong foundation. You are about to create an amazing life you absolutely LOVE, simply by applying the strategies I have shared with you so far in this book, BUT it is critical that we do a little foundational inspection before you get too far ahead of yourself.

I don't know about you, but in my pre-OMG life there were days I sat in my big ol'chair in the living room totally stunned, flipping channels for hours staring right though the TV. Or, I stretched out on the couch with my body aching so much the thought of getting up to exercise was totally out of the question. Even then, had I possessed the greatest of ideas and had all the tricks I needed to create a life I loved, I didn't have the energy or the mental focus to do jack-shit. I was sluggish and unhealthy. So, I had to start from the ground up. I had to create a foundation for bliss and wellness. I had to create a foundation for focus. I had to have a way for celebrating my progress to keep myself motivated. I had to quiet the distractions so I could visualize all the wonderful things I wanted for my family and me!

I had to create a foundation for this OMG life so that once I had it, when life's little curve balls came my way I would possess the resources and strength to say, "Not this time! You are NOT knocking me on my ass again!"

The quality of your self-care forms the foundation that you are going to build the rest of your life upon. Just like any building with a faulty foundation, if your self-care is poor or non-existent, the life you build on it can only handle so much stress before it crumples like a house of cards. Problems can manifest themselves in all forms, such as: migraines, fatigue, inability to handle stress, anger, weight gain or weight loss, poor appetite, anxiety, unexplained pain, relationship conflicts, unhappiness, emotional eating, illness, and so on.

So let's address some basics before I set you free!

Chapter 11:
CREATING THE FOUNDATION FOR
BLISS AND WELLNESS

Personal Training is very rewarding work. But addressing physical wellness is only one part of anyone's life as you can see from the Reality Check activity you did earlier. If one part of a person's life is out of whack, the other pieces suffer.

When I started training clients they would see results in their energy levels, waistlines, and their emotional well-being. They'd noticed they could handle stress more effectively and that when they worked out, they didn't want to eat poorly. Their new state of wellness supported better choices! Things were good. They felt better. They were excited about the changes they were making.

But then, just as they were making progress, the wheels would fly off and they would begin faltering, making excuses, and giving up. Or, something would happen in their life that would knock them off their feet and they didn't appear to have the skills to cope with any stressors beyond the regular day-to-day stuff. They had no buffer, no reserve, and no coping strategies. I kept asking myself, "What is really going on here?" I was keen to learning more about how I could help my clients by addressing their needs more holistically.

It became apparent through some heart-to-heart exchanges (through snot bubbles and Kleenex boxes) that some clients were falling off the wagon just as the greatest progress could be made because other parts of their lives were out of control. For example, Sara always worked hard and pushed her workouts to the max. Then suddenly, she started showing up with a negative cloud hanging over her and she lacked effort in her workouts. Turns out, Sara's husband had started making snide remarks about her "fat ass" just as she started to lose significant weight and feel good. He asked her straight out why she was even bothering because she would end up failing like she had previously. Sara's little voice started to agree and she began to wonder if it was worth it. She had removed junk food from the pantry to keep it out of the house so she wouldn't have it on hand, and he replaced it and would ask her if she wanted any. Sara couldn't control his behavior or his reactions to her progress and she was confused and hurt by his deliberate attempts to sabotage her success.

What Sara had to learn was that while she couldn't control his behavior, she could control her reactions to his behaviors. By changing her reactions to his behaviors, she began to change the dynamic between them. When he said hurtful things, rather than slink off to the bedroom and cry alone, she asked him why he would say such things, "Don't you want me to be healthy and happy?" When he offered her foods that were not in line with her goals, she reminded him, "I am doing awesome. I don't want to fall off the wagon so please do not offer me foods you know I do not want to eat. I'd love your support."

She kept inviting him to join her or to try new recipes. We discussed that his behavior was a reflection of what could be going on inside of him as a result of her success. She wanted to be healthy and feel beautiful. He felt threatened. She admitted he often said he felt unhealthy and maybe he wanted her success for himself. She gave him a bit of space to get his head around his own issues and she kept on pushing to be successful to show him that his words were not going to stop her success. **She was reaching a crossroads between choosing to fail to satisfy his insecurities or rising to shine despite them.**

She opted to SHINE and reminded herself that she was not responsible for his happiness. She began to see how having one part of her life out of whack was influencing her success in other areas and understood her relationship conflict needed to be addressed. Her husband came around after lots of discussion and decided he needed to be healthy as well. While he hasn't jumped fully on board, he is supportive of the food choices and her workout schedules and instead of making mean comments, he shares how much better he feels and how happy he is that they are making changes together. Sara had to lead and being the leader isn't always easy.

As I continued to have contact with clients in person and through online training groups, it became blatantly clear that many people didn't know the basics about the benefits of self-care (and I don't mean the simple stuff like brush your teeth and comb your hair). Looking back, when I was at my most overwhelmed neither did I. I just pushed harder and faster in a feeble attempt to keep up. I put my wellness aside and my long-term health in jeopardy. I became less effective, more miserable, and drifted into darker places.

Life moves fast. Technology has made us easy to find, track, interrupt, and the emails and text messages that can find us anywhere always seem so bloody urgent. If you have kids, you might feel pressure to give them every opportunity you possibly can: soccer, baseball, football, swimming, hockey, music or the arts. You might work all day to come home to a self-imposed extra-curricular frenzy with every night of the week full of quick meals, fast hellos, and rushed goodnights. Living life fast leaves no time to decompress or to connect with loved ones because everyone is flying out the door in different directions.

If you do not have kids but you work in a competitive work environment, you might feel the pressure to always do more, give more, and be more to keep your job. And if you have both a competitive job and a family, God help you!

But, there is one job that many people forget all about. It is the beautiful work of taking care of ourselves.

Please, let me remind you that YOU are the most important person in YOUR life. It all starts with you. You have to take the time to care for yourself because that is no one else's job. If you destroy yourself or your wellness because you do not take the time to address your own well-being FIRST, what good will you be to the people who need you most when you have driven yourself into the ground with exhaustion and neglect? **If you need permission to care about yourself, I am giving it to you now!**

Park the guilt at the doorstep. Hell, throw it out with the trash! You should NEVER feel badly for tending to your own needs! A better, happier, well-balanced you makes every relationship and exchange you have in a given day richer and sweeter! If you are so stressed out that you are unbearable to be around, how is that helpful to anyone? And, how does it feel to live inside that body and mind that can't keep up to the demands you continuously push upon it? You cannot keep giving if you never stop to refuel.

Physical Wellness
The world sees your exterior first, but what you project outwardly is deeply connected to what you feel inwardly, so let's start there.

Look in the mirror and imagine yourself twenty pounds leaner, or toner, or more fit and strong. Imagine how much better you would feel about everything – how you moved, how your clothes felt and how much easier it would be to carry laundry up the stairs. Even if twenty pounds didn't take you to your ideal weight, if you learned sustainable habits that could take you to a healthier life, wouldn't it be worth it? I changed my eating habits but I didn't just jump on someone else's bandwagon. I learned to try new things and love the foods I discovered were healthy. Small changes, over time, equaled HUGE benefits. While I wouldn't march on stage for a bikini competition, I am so much healthier.

Had I not taken control I likely would be eighty pounds overweight and diabetic. I'm predisposed to diabetes because I have a condition called PCOS. This condition is a leading cause of infertility and is associated with additional conditions, including an increased risk of endometrial cancer, depression, anxiety, heart disease, hypertension, and lipid abnormalities. In other words, I didn't have the choice to neglect myself anymore if I wanted to be here to raise my children. But I didn't need to get this unhealthy before I did something about it either. Sometimes I wonder if I felt I needed permission to care about myself. I am so much more knowledgeable about eating and working out and I am tenfold richer for investing in myself like I have. If there is one thing you need to know, it is that YOU ARE WORTH THE INVESTMENT.

Your body wants you to move it. People always use the excuse that they don't have time to exercise. Do the math. You have twenty-four hours in a day just like everyone else. If you devote one hour (or even thirty minutes) a day to moving in a manner that you enjoy (enjoyment is KEY), that is $1/24^{th}$ of your day. That is only four percent of YOUR day (or two percent) devoted to what has been proven to extend your life, increase you ability to deal with stress, decrease incident of disease, enhance your mood, and increase your overall well-being. Don't you think you DESERVE to claim ownership over at least four percent of your day? I certainly think you do!

If you still don't think you have the time, you are just not ready to be honest with yourself. You have to make the choice to make the time. I can tell a client exactly what they need to do, but they have to CHOOSE to do it! I cannot do the work for them. As a single mom, I managed to find the time to work fulltime and train for Ironman Canada Triathlon in both 2008 and 2010. I also had one or both of my kids ninety percent of the time so I had to work around my responsibilities so I could still be a good mother and get them to their own activities. (I know there are many other single parents doing some pretty creative things to make similar things happen). **We ALL have the same 24 hours in a day, but we make different choices about how we spend it.**

Many mornings I was up at four or five to get in one of the workouts I had scheduled for that day. Some nights I was up a little later to make sure a second workout got completed before a new day arrived. My choice. I told myself that I was not permitted to watch any TV unless I was on my bike trainer, which gave me motivation to bike! I did some running workouts around soccer fields and took the joking from other parents in stride. Sure, I might have looked like a crazy girl running intervals in back alleys and up park hills, but I was also paying attention to what my kids were doing so I could cheer them on as they did their thing. In my books, it was win-win. I often wondered what I was teaching my children because I know they were watching.

One day, I had a training run to do and my daughter wanted to go to the barn for a summer trail ride but she had no one to go with. I wanted to be fair to her and welcomed the challenge of a different opportunity to run. So, I volunteered to take my run to the trails out behind the barn and told her that I would run while she rode her horse. I would be the "lead horse" because I didn't want her out on the trails alone.

I knew it would be a challenge to run the horse trails, but didn't really have any knowledge of the terrain because I had never been back there. It was super hot, so I threw on my brightly colored Lululemons (hardly western riding gear), and she threw on her boots. She saddled up Prince. I tied up my running shoes and off we went. Little did I know, that I would come face to face with an unsuspecting group of people on horseback out for a trail-ride. There I was decked out in Lulu, with my daughter and her horse hot on my heels, running way outside my comfort zone because I thought Prince might actually bite my ear. (He really thought I was the lead horse.)

Every step was a struggle running up and over the sand dunes, dodging gopher holes, and random horse droppings. The mosquitos were feasting on my poorly protected skin. I was a purple, panting mess and I ran right into the group cresting the same hill from the opposite direction. Yes, I am sure they thought I was a complete nut job. Oh well! My daughter got her trail ride and I got my run in. In fact, the challenging sandy terrain made the run fun and it pushed me to new performance levels. My daughter enjoyed it as well because she playfully urged Prince to run a little faster just to see me struggle. It was a new adventure and it sure beat the same old training run I had planned on doing. Mission accomplished!

People who dread exercise just haven't discovered what works for them. You shouldn't punish yourself with exercise; reward yourself with it! It should be something you look forward to doing. Try a fun activity like ZUMBA or a Mud Run with friends. Take up walking at a good clip and talking with a cherished friend. My sister used to complain we never saw one another so I told her she should start running with me. We ran-walked her first four-kilometers so it was enjoyable for her but after that she was hooked. She went on to run races and loved them. You have to enjoy what you do or it will never be a long-term lifestyle change.

But let's not fool ourselves. It isn't just about the exercise. Yes, physical activity will make you feel better almost immediately. I mean you can't be happy if you are lethargic, sedentary, and cross-eyed tired. Plus, feeling healthy and strong makes you happier and a healthy dose of exercise-induced endorphins doesn't hurt either! When it comes to fitness you have to expend energy to gain energy. But sometimes there is a lag in the energy pick up and you can find yourself thinking that the first few weeks are going to actually kill you. Providing you do not have any underlying medical issues (which is why it's always prudent to check with your GP before starting an exercise program), movement will not kill you. Once you get over the initial hump, your body will thank you by putting a little more pep in your step, and you will begin appreciating what physical activity can do for you.

And please do not misunderstand me: you do not have to be a professional athlete, compete in an Ironman, hop on stage at a figure competition, or participate in a Crossfit Challenge. You just need to start moving. A solid walking program could make a huge impact on your quality of life. Join a group class or grab a couple of friends and head to the gym. A quick and efficient bodyweight workout that you can do at home could restore your core strength and posture to help alleviate that nagging back pain. If your knees hurt, try Aquasize. I find that when I do not move my body it starts to get stiff and sore. I always feel better after I have done something, even if it is a walk at the dog park! Just start with something little and build from there.

To truly create a strong foundation for bliss, you need to address several other factors. As we move ahead, we will look briefly at the role that sleep, nutrition, basic care, downtime, and celebrating your progress plays in establishing this foundation.

Sleep

Research shows that sleep deprivation leads to critical changes in our hormone levels. Two hormones that are impacted by the quality of sleep are ghrelin and leptin. Ghrelin is the hormone that tells you to eat, and you have MORE of it when you are sleep-deprived. That means, you have the urge to eat more. Sleep deprivation also decreases your levels of leptin and leptin tells you when to STOP eating. Therefore, when you are overtired you never get the message to stop eating.

These hormones, when disrupted, tell your brain to eat more and never stop. Hormone disruption also encourages you to make poor food choices. Coupled with that is excess levels of cortisol (stress hormone) in your body can make you fat, interfere with weight loss, and ultimately lead to disease. Sounds like a recipe for a disaster doesn't it?

Adequate sleep helps stabilize important hormones, helps heal and rejuvenate, and readies you for the coming day. Oh, and it feels great! (If only working out was this easy.) So ladies, go to fricking sleep! Stop trying to do "just one more thing" before bed. There is always "one more thing to do." Yes, I am talking to YOU!

Oh, and another thing, have you ever snapped at someone? Ha, bet you have! Let's not forget how cheerful you are when you are sleep deprived. Everyone loves to be around the bitchy, half-baked zombie at work don't they? And, your kids and spouse love it when you turn on them like the Wicked Witch of the West for asking where the apples are! Your BFF calls you on your mood swings too, doesn't she? Yes, it ALL begins with sleep. Start there. You won't be sorry!

You ARE What You Eat

We might be exhausted and busy but we still need to eat. We might have families that need to be fed, too. What you eat is critical to how you feel.

When I was most overwhelmed, I grabbed the quickest options I could find. They usually lived in the freezer section and had a long list of ingredients I couldn't pronounce: a chemical storm wrapped up in a pretty little box. Since I was the only one cooking, it was appealing to me that I could throw something in the oven while I did the other chores that needed to be done. I was a processed food junkie. I thought "natural" and "low-fat" meant it was good for me! I believed the marketing on the package design. Imagine that! This is one reason we need to accept responsibility for educating ourselves about food because packages lie. It's all marketing. That model on the frozen food you just bought doesn't eat that crap because if she did, she wouldn't look like that.

I bought into the hype and the "processed healthy" food movement. If I ate now the way I did back in my WTF days, my insides would have nothing to do with me. My body can no longer tolerate the heavily-processed, greasy, or pretend foods. I get sick. Anytime I cheat (because sometimes I do), I am reminded why I prefer to eat clean.

Anyone for a honey sandwich and a coke? How about a super-sized Micky D Meal? Or, KFC with some gravy and fries? No wait, the ultimate quick meal: KD and hotdogs! Nutrition is key to controlling other aspects of your life. It is your fuel. You are a sexy little race car, so don't put swamp water in your tank!

Fuel up with premium foods. Simple rules to follow include eating nutritionally dense whole foods (the ones without labels, like apples or raw nuts), and chowing down on appropriate portion sizes. Eat when you are paying attention. Chew your food and actually taste it! Novel idea, but consider sitting down to eat and have a conversation with that kid over there. Your child is worth the investment, too.

Avoid the junk foods. Chips, pops, cookies, baked goods, and quick pre-packaged snacks only lead to those crash and burn cycles you want to avoid. Shop for your week's groceries on a full, satisfied stomach or else you will end up with seven-layer dip, Piggy Puffs (used to be my favorite snack, and yes that is deep fried pig fat), and Oreo cookies in your cart. Stick to the perimeter of the shop where the veggies, fruits, and lean proteins live. Hit the farmer's markets to buy fresh and in season. You will find the market food tastes so much better, which can help you enjoy eating clean even more. Don't believe me? Compare a carrot bought from a local farmer to one from the big chain grocery store (or let your kids) and you will never go back. Market grown carrots taste like candy compared to what big chain grocers sell!

Pay attention to what you put in your mouth and ask yourself, "What will this do for me?" That one question alone will have you putting half the crap down before it hits your lips and then your hips!

With physical movement and nutrition covered, let's move on to basic care.

Basic Care

This may seem a little harsh and for most, totally not necessary. However, for the few of you that are sitting there in your old sweat pants hiding behind raggedy old T-shirts and hoping to go unnoticed, I am just going to run over basic care concepts because when we are suffering in our mindsets, this basic care stuff can take a backseat and fall right off our radar.

You know when you have the flu and you are in bed for days? You feel greasy and grotesque. Ever notice how the longer you lay around without showering the worse you feel? That's all I am getting at here. Girlfriend, shower daily. Brush your teeth, floss and give a good rinse. Tend to your stray facial hair, your skincare, and shape your brows. Get your haircut regularly and keep it clean and brushed. Wear clean clothes that fit your body type. I lived in sweat pants and large tee shirts all the while I blossomed into miserable momma underneath. I just wanted to hide, to deny, and to pretend things were fine. They were not fine and denial got me absolutely nowhere.

Wear make-up, if that's your thing. Just care daily for yourself so you feel fresh and clean. Why? Because it shows others that you care about yourself, that you feel worthy, and that you haven't given up even if your life currently sucks. And, no one is going to tell you if you look like shit, even if you do. They also are unlikely to tell you if you stink, because they don't want to hurt your feelings or come off as rude but lack of self care CAN and WILL alienate you from others.

Basic care can be tough for people who are truly suffering but please, please, please try to care for yourself so that you don't create obstacles for yourself. As Terri Cole says, "There is nothing impressive about treating your body and your life like crap!" Nuff said.

Downtime

With the pressure to do all and be all, it is great to teach your kids about choices and priorities. Let them make the choices about which activities they want to participate in given YOUR guidelines. We can't do it all. If your life is crazy hectic, consider booking one night a week that belongs to you to do with whatever you please. Could be a night in with a great book, a night out with your friends, or salsa dancing (even if you have to guzzle root beer schnapps in the parking lot to get up the guts to go in the first few times— no wait it was Yagermeister— no wait it was both). It doesn't matter what you do with that time, but it must belong to you and you must be in control of what you do with it. Schedule it in your phone. If your phone is like my phone at all, it's beeping and pinging non-stop, so why not make one of those beeps a reminder to take the night off and enjoy yourself!

As September rolls around each year, I start my scheduling with my kids' extracurricular interests. I find out when their classes will be and I schedule them in. This year, my daughter gets Wednesday and Thursday evenings for horse lessons and my son gets Tuesday and Sunday for cadets. With only one driver in the house right now I need to think about who I can drop off where and when, just like you do, right? Saturday, my daughter often rides again and sometimes my son has cadet obligations. This leaves Friday and Monday. Since the weekends are usually hectic, I claim Monday as MY day. Friday we leave open to negotiations. Last year, I claimed Thursdays because that worked better but life changes, so you need to be prepared to as well.

Acknowledge and Celebrate Progress

Self-care behaviors that become fully integrated into your life long term usually happen in baby steps over a period of time and not huge leaps all of a sudden. But, baby steps and slight adjustments OVER TIME can make a HUGE impact on your life! So don't be ashamed if you start small. Just start!

For example, consider the woman who decided she needed to get more regular quality sleep to help her fight fatigue. She started going to bed an hour earlier than usual and found the quality of her sleep improved drastically, often waking up before her alarm went off. After a couple weeks she was feeling invigorated, and she was then able to get up half hour earlier every day to take a brisk walk before going to work. She felt this cleared her head and made her feel more prepared to face the day at the office because she had a little time to think about it before she got there. She then noticed she didn't crave her soft drinks anymore and she swapped them out for lemon water and green tea. One day she was getting dressed and her clothes were fitting differently so she jumped on the scale to see that these new choices had her down twelve pounds in about six weeks.

She thought a bit about refining her diet and decided that she wanted to try cutting out as much processed food as she could because she had heard that eating clean, whole foods could help people deal with migraines. She spent one weekend purging her pantry and freezer and prepared a few new recipes she had come across that she had wanted to try. Within three months, her migraines had improved significantly and she started to notice how sick she felt when she made poor food choices. None of the changes she made to her life created ANY hardships at all and these small changes, made consistently over time, took her to a totally different lifestyle and state of wellness. She told me she couldn't believe she didn't do it sooner, but she also thought it would be way harder and she would feel deprived and grouchy. Instead, she says she feels energetic, positive and a decade younger.

Small changes made consistently over time trump big changes in terms of sustainability. Lives do not always need an overhaul; some just need a slight tweaking. If you are overwhelmed, focusing on basic care is a perfect place to start so you have the energy to take it up a notch when you feel steadier on your feet. Creating an OMG life is all about finding YOUR sweet spot!

My main message here is that if you are always making the best choice for yourself in any given situation, wellness will follow as a result. Avoid the pressure to be a certain weight or size and make the best choices you can on a consistent basis so that the things you do change in your lifestyle are sustainable long term. Otherwise, when life throws you one of its curve balls and it all hits the fan, you will find yourself up the creek without a paddle once again! And ladies, when you make progress, acknowledge it. Don't belittle it and pretend it doesn't matter. It matters because you matter. I get emails all the time, "I ran for fifteen minutes today!" "I did it! I feel great!" and I am eager to reply with a heartfelt congratulations because I know these ladies are working their asses off to create that OMG life and they deserve the recognition for each step they take!

SWIFTKICK TIP: Start from where you are, but START!

Write down three things you can change right now that will lend themselves to increasing your level of self-care. If you are broke, create a list that requires little monetary investment. Some suggestions that cost nothing include scheduling more sleep, painting your toenails, or having coffee with a friend (connection and care). Cindy reminded me, "not only do you tend to dress a little better (no sweatpants) for coffee with a friend, it is also the cheapest form of therapy a women can get for under five bucks!" I would have to agree with her on that one!

Consider preparing healthier meals, going for a walk outside (fresh air and movement), and purging your closet of clothes that no longer fit into your new dream life! For an extra large deposit to the Karma account, donate the clothing to a family in need or an organization that helps women going through hard times. You will feel good helping others while helping yourself.

Now that you have created your own list of self-care items, make them real. Schedule them into your calendar and Tweet me your list (@SwiftKickFitnes). Use your phone to set alarms for bedtime and go to bed. (Yes, I am serious). Or, set a daily reminder to take a twenty-minute walk and then stick to these plans! Last year, I had a date with myself every Thursday evening during the academic year and that is the day of the week I save for myself. My main message is that just thinking about changing your life isn't going to do anything unless you ACT. START doing the things that you have identified will change your life. Girl, you got this! Now get moving!

Chapter 12:
BEING YOURSELF

Once you address the basics of exercise, sleep, nutrition and self-care so you can build that sturdy foundation, it's time to take a look at your life below the physical surface. Let's check in with your heart and see how your emotional life is doing.

The first step to becoming emotionally healthy is to love your real self. Really love and value WHO YOU ARE. Remember, I said I would strip you down and build you back up from the head down and the heart out? Here we go.

You need to love your REAL self for so many reasons. Loving exactly who you are makes your life so much less of a struggle. You can always work on being your best YOU, but love who you are now so that you can respect yourself enough to be able to make the best choices for yourself at any given moment! You are WORTHY of such goodness. Do not punish yourself if there are things you want to change about yourself, love yourself enough to put the effort in to making the change. Please do not break your own spirit by hating who you are now.

Being authentic also permits a much deeper connection with other people. In fact, connection that is authentic is on an entirely different plane and because of that, it leads to entirely different emotional, mental, and spiritual experiences. When you are completely yourself and you are able to be real and raw with someone you know you are safe with, the experiences can be astounding. As I have come to know first hand, the richest lives are lived by the people who allow themselves to be completely vulnerable.

When being open and vulnerable you have experiences that are incredibly powerful because there are no obstacles in the way and no issues that dilute the strength and power of whatever is taking place. Yes, it takes the ability to risk being hurt when you put yourself in this place, but the rewards are huge. While I wouldn't throw myself into the streets and risk being totally vulnerable with just any one, each time I have risked being open, I have learned the deepest of lessons.

It is also important to address the fact that a series of horrible events could have brought you to your WTF life and you may not be ready to be open with anyone. You may be just getting back on your feet. If that is the case, start with being vulnerable with yourself first. Be kind, forgiving, and patient with yourself. Really care for yourself like you would a close friend. Remember, healing happens from the inside out: No one can do the work for you on this one. If you are hurting and finding it difficult to overcome the pain, stay the course. Come to terms with what is hurting you, voice it, call it out, and name it as specifically as you can. The goal here is to take care of yourself until you are at the point where you are strong enough to be ready to be open again.

If you feel you are not good enough (that the person who got the job is better than you, that you are not enough or you are deficient in some way, that the other woman is better, that you are not a good mother, partner, or friend), you will have to eventually deal with that sense of deficiency AT THE CORE before you can move forward into bliss. Skipping that step (and so many do as they try to medicate themselves with material possessions, drugs, sex, or alcohol), will have you moving on and getting a new boyfriend, new job, or a new car in an attempt to make that feeling go away. It won't. You have to change the thinking. You will still have that feeling of deficiency because you cannot fix it with things or other people. And, if your mindset isn't addressed, it is hard to be real because the hurt holds you back from being vulnerable.

You are enough. Be a force to be reckoned with by being real. This is your power source. It is your authenticity that will set you free.

We are often uncomfortable when we create space in our lives until we connect to who we really are. Cindy shared her reflection with me after a recent relationship came to an end. "After a break up, whether wanted or not, there is a void. The knee jerk reaction is to fill it quickly and that is a mistake. This is the time you should focus on yourself. Organize drawers, purge, and do all the things that you didn't have time for before."

Change is good. Being dynamic and always changing is the richest way to live your life. You don't need stuff to be happy; you need to be real so that everything you do is in tune with who you truly are at your core. Once you know who you are (and you WILL know because it feels so fantastic to live in that space, truly it is key to the OMG life), you can figure out WHAT you really want. You create the mindset, build the foundation, and then you align it with your heartfelt goodness and you have it girlfriend, you have the OMG Life. I know! I am ready to cry, too!

Vision Boards – The Key to Having It All

Our minds are amazing tools. They possess the capacity to do things we cannot even fathom. We use a small portion of them to move through day-to-day life, but there is so much more to the human mind that remains a mystery. How can we tap into the power of our minds to help move us in the directions of a kickass OMG life?

I'm glad you asked. Did you know that your conscious and subconscious minds often have different agendas? Did you know that even if your conscious mind has said "X will be this way," that your subconscious mind can go against what you have consciously planned and you may not even be aware of this conflict? The subconscious mind runs 24/7, whereas the conscious mind is only running when YOU have instructed it to do so. Therefore, you must bring your subconscious mind onboard with your conscious mind so that the two can work in alignment and not in conflict. Who knew? I certainly didn't! This stuff should be taught in high school!

You have likely heard people talk about vision boards. To the person who is unfamiliar with the power of vision boards and the philosophy behind them, their creation looks like an adult craft class. But vision boards and visualization strategies are extremely powerful tools because they allow your subconscious mind the experience it needs in order to support life change. Even though these experiences are "pretend" and have not taken place in real life. Yet. Please let me explain.

Your conscious thoughts are the thoughts you control. "I like that dress." "Oh that salad looks good." "Wow, look at that chocolate cake." "Oh my gosh what a cute baby!" "That girl looks fit, I want to be just like her!" You are aware of them happening and in control of them.

Meanwhile, your subconscious mind runs in the background, like an operating system on your computer (same idea as default behaviors). You are not aware of what your subconscious mind is doing or how its actions are impacting your life. Your subconscious thoughts are also often influenced by your internal belief systems (as we discussed in "It's Time to Get Off"). These belief systems have been created over time as a result of the experiences you have had to date. But, here is the thing. While you may be consciously thinking "I like that dress." "Oh that salad looks good." "Wow, look at that chocolate cake." "Oh my gosh what a cute baby!" "That girl looks fit, I want to be just like her!" your subconscious mind makes it sound more like this:

"I like that dress." *"Too bad your fat ass would never fit in it."* "Oh that salad looks good." *"Well dig in, princess, because the desserts need to be off limits!"* "Wow, look at that chocolate cake." *"Oh wait a minute, what about your diet plan? You are such a loser! You are never going to lose the weight you want. You have no willpower!"* "Oh my gosh what a cute baby!" *"You have been trying for years to conceive, God must know you would be a horrible mother!"* "That girl looks fit, I want to be just like her!" *"Spend any more time at the buffet and that is never going to happen!"*

Having both the conscious and the subconscious minds running at the same time can be counter-productive if they are not aligned. However, if your conscious and subconscious minds ARE aligned, and both support your dreams and desires, the duo can be seriously powerful. Let's align the two minds using vision boards and visualization!

Minds Aligned: Cooperative Visualization

Your mind, as totally awesome as it is, has a few quirks we can use to our advantage. As Dr. Maxwell Maltz states, "Change occurs not by intellect, and not by intelligence; change is brought about by experience" and lucky for us, our subconscious mind doesn't know the difference between real experience and imagined experience! For that exact reason, visualization and imagining your dreams coming true over and over again teaches your brain exactly that is possible. As you get more and more comfortable with your visualized goals coming true and what you would see, hear, feel and experience there – in your visualizations – your brain accepts that you have already experienced it! It is at this point that any possible previously sabotaging behaviors begin to disappear because your brain believes fully that you have already experienced this success!

Since we do not have the luxury of a lifetime of experiences, let's create them. Let's play pretend. Let's visualize. Let's collect images of the things we love. Let's activate our imaginations just like kids do when they dream of being superwoman, doctors, mothers, horse trainers, lawyers, firefighters, dolphin trainers, or the people who cure cancer! When you visualize your goals and dreams, you trick your subconscious into believing it has already had the experience and then when you begin to make it happen, your subconscious mind isn't slamming down sabotaging behaviors and limiting belief systems. Instead it says, "Hey, we have done this before, and it feels awesome to be doing it again!" No alarm bells get set off by your subconscious mind and you increase your comfort zone significantly which allows you to do things that previously would have made you terrified and anxious!

How truly cool is that? It's like magic.

Visualization in Sports

When I was training for Ironman Canada 2010, I wrote out my splits for the 3.8 km open water swim, the 180 km bike and the 42.2km run on a sticky note and placed the note on my computer monitor at work. The sticky note really became a part of the décor. I looked at those numbers daily – sometimes I stopped and thought about them consciously for a minute and "visualized" or imagined the race in detail, and sometimes I saw the sticky note but paid it no attention. That note stayed on my monitor almost an entire training year.

When I returned from Ironman Canada, I saw the sticky note and it stopped me in my tracks. For as much as I had consciously looked at it over the past year, I forgot about it! Guess what? Swim split – bang on!

Bike time – one minute off! Run split – four minutes off. I was kind of astonished that I was staring at what actually took place on race day! It was like I ordered up my race dreams and they were delivered (yes, there was work involved). Given that Ironman can be up to a seventeen-hour day, to be a few minutes off on a split is nothing. I also used this tactic as a young competitive swimmer and it brought me great success. If you can see it, you can believe it.

Now it is your turn to figure out where you are headed and communicate that to your brain as EXPERIENCES through visualization.

SWIFTKICK TIP: Create Your Vision Board

Make a vision board so you know exactly where you are headed. Cut out pictures, quotes, doodles, and anything else that needs to go on that vision board. Glue the pictures in a collage and place it somewhere you will see it daily. Imagine yourself in the images. When you are visualizing yourself there, activate as many senses as possible: What does it feel like to be there? How does it smell? Taste? What do you hear? If you can SEE yourself being there, and FEEL yourself being there, you will get there! A bonus of knowing exactly what you want is that you become more open to the opportunities around you that will help get you there! And, put your dreams out there because people genuinely want to help others and they can't help you if they don't know what you need help with! When I verbalized I wanted to author a book, friends started supporting me, and suddenly people I never knew prior popped into my life with skills and advice to help the process begin. The universe takes care of the how and you just have to know what YOU want!

Don't get all tangled up in the logistics of "how" the dream will come to be, believe it just will. Make the creation of your vision board a "night out" with the gals. Have everyone bring healthy snacks and beverages and chat the night away about your dreams and where you are headed! It's energizing, motivating and fun! You might have friends and acquaintances right now that have what you need to make a dream come true and they would LOVE to help you but they don't know what you dream about. So share! Verbalize it! Give your dreams life!

Visualization and imagining your dreams coming true over and over again teaches your brain that exactly what you are imagining IS possible. As you get more and more comfortable with your visualized goals coming true and what you would see, hear, feel and experience there when it happens in real life, your brain accepts that you have already **experienced** it! Remember as Maltz states, "Change is brought about through experience." If this is true (and I believe it is) your **imagination** provides that experience needed to initiate the change you so desire!

If you have ever been very close to realizing your goals only to have "something" prevent it – perhaps a behavior you never really noticed in yourself before – this is often a result of your mind trying to stay where it is comfortable. Your mind loves the state of homeostasis. If you train your brain to think beyond your comfort zones, by utilizing your imagination, the behaviors that get in the way magically begin to disappear! Abracadabra!

SWIFTKICK TIP: Setting Intention from a Fully Invested Place
In this commonly used life coaching activity, you are working to create one statement that fully captures what your intentions are for your life. You will know it when you write it. It will sit peacefully with you. You will get excited, not afraid. This is a process so it can involve a few do-overs, modifications, and so on.

1. **You do KNOW what you want.** Sometimes fear is so strong we think we do not know what we want. Sometimes we fear judgment so strongly we don't let our own thoughts come through. Quiet yourself. Sit still. Verbalizing your goals can be scary and real and super exciting! Do not say you do not know. Believe

fully that you do and have faith in the process of this coming to you. If you are struggling, focus on your feelings. How does an idea feel to you? Feelings don't lie.

2. **Wishy-Washy Non-Committal Language Won't Do!** Commit to your LIFE! Your intentions are made of powerful words that tell you exactly what you WILL be doing, what you will have, or who you will be. Not what you "sorta might" do if the wind blows the right way on the perfect day in December.

   - "My intention is to remove the obstacles from my life so that I can focus all my energy on the things that matter to me."
   - "My intention is to get clear about the next step I am taking in my life."
   - "My intention is to enjoy being alone with myself and learn how to love myself."

Just a note about why we write statements like those above. If I write, "I love myself" and I do not currently love myself, my body instantly calls bullshit. It feels like a lie. If I write, "My intention is to love myself for all my unique gifts." That feels better. It is true, because that is my intention even if it is not my reality at this moment.

3. **Intentions are not written in stone**. Once you settle into the processes of becoming more and more aware or your default settings and your automated behaviors, more clarity may come to you and you may find that you need to modify your intentions to make them feel right with the newly recharged person you are becoming. Not only is this ok, I encourage you to get increasingly more specific. **This is how the OMG begins to emerge and form and bloom. You will feel it!**

My Intention Is...

With your intentions sketched out, we move on to discuss why what you focus on expands. It will be a great reminder for you to focus on the things you want (so they can expand), not what you don't want (because that can expand, too)!

Chapter 13:
THE POWER OF FOCUS

Now that you have cleared the decks of all the crud in your life, you will begin to feel an increased sense of energy and ability to focus. Focus is your secret weapon! As you release the things that do not serve you (silly little energy-sucking parasites) you will have much more space in your physical environment, your mind, and in your heart to focus on what you do desire. You will become aware of how much energy you wasted on things that didn't serve your intentions. Once you do, there is no going back. Now that you have all this new energy and focus, it is time to put it to use for creating this OMG life you are seeking.

More space. More Energy. More focus.
While I have already talked about how focus and fear work together, it is time to realize how focus can impact other areas of your life. My weight-loss journey was a perfect example of this. I saw "that" hideous before picture that told me I was now officially fat. It kicked off a glorious WTF Moment.

I was donning my old lady floral tankini and I was partially jammed into an inflatable beach tube. It was really one of those moments where you are like, "Holy shit. This is out of control. No more." I was officially fat. Why the hell was everyone keeping it a secret? Why didn't anyone tell me? Oh, I know. "Hey, you are fat!" wouldn't have gone over very well. True to any WTF Moment, I was educated and I accepted responsibility for letting life get the best of me! My inside voice was having a field day: "Put your big girl panties on because you have work to do girl. Getting more and more unhealthy is not an option!"

Although, I am sure I was fat for some time before *officially* realizing it myself. I, like many of you, was just too busy dealing with my day-to-day life to pay attention (lack of awareness) to my expanding size or too stressed to relax long enough to take stock of my current situation. Anyway, once I saw that picture and decided NO more, I was dead set on committing to a change. (Remember, this is the power of a WTF Moment). I knew I wasn't going to just "try" and see what would happen; I was really committing myself to whatever it took to get the job done. I got laser-focused on what I wanted. (Remember, what you focus on expands and grows and becomes powerful. It gets all your energy, too.)

Because I had this focus, my energy was funneled to the things that would move me closer to my goals, not further away. TV time didn't matter anymore. Sleep, clean eating, and a hard workout did. I planned meals, workouts, and sleep. I had sticky notes all over the house reminding me how awesome I was. I planned for success. I fully understood that if I failed to plan these things I needed for my personal success that I was, by default, planning to fail!

Water the Grass!

Christine Kane reminded me that "your energy flows where your attention goes" so give the things you want to grow your love and attention. You have heard the saying, "The grass is always greener on the other side of the fence," right? Well, not really. The grass is greener where you water it!!

"Comparison is the thief of joy." ~ Theodore Roosevelt

Some of the most unhappy people are the ones that spend their days comparing their lives to the lives of others -- over there on the other side of the ol'fence. The only problem with this is that you have NO clue what their lives are really like behind closed doors. Even if you think you do, you don't. So what you compare yourself to is your own idea about how great their life is and you can't possibly know. You do, however, know exactly what your ENTIRE life is like so it's a pretty unfair comparison that is going to leave you feeling like a big bag o' shit.

I call this type of comparison the "glory reel" because you hold yourself up against another person's highlights, successes and accomplishments (all their glory) but you show up with all your baggage, struggles, and failures because you know yourself intimately. Take Facebook for example, how many people post their most human side on their feed? It doesn't feel right that they post, "My husband pissed me off today and my kids are driving me nuts." Instead you might get a post like, "Was having a bad day but turned it around and feel awesome!" What is the truth? Also, I have heard people say that Facebook posts can also get people who know you thinking more about your problems and anything negative you might post, which shifts their energy, too. I bring you back to "Not my circus, not my monkeys."

AND, this silly comparison game, or keeping up with the Jones' gets ALL your focus, and therefore, all your precious energy! Where does that leave your dreams? Yep, you got it, sister. Lack of focus leaves your dreams sitting on the curb waiting for you to get your act together!

No More Shiny Things
Ever hose the winter grime off your driveway? Using the nozzle you can adjust the flow into a really focused jet of water and it moves all the dirt and crud quickly. If you open the nozzle and put it on another

setting, the water fans out, the pressure fades, and you are not nearly as effective at moving things. Think of this when you think of focus. Quite simply, the more concentrated your efforts, the greater the results.

A little twist on that is that you could have the nozzle on the right setting but maybe you keep on looking up at all the shiny things that keep on walking by. Every time you look up, you lose momentary control and shoot that water off into the grass or into the dirt you have already moved and you splatter it all over the driveway. Now you have to start again!

When I take this story and apply it to daily life, I think about all the little things that try to lure my focus away from the task at hand. Clutter at the front door that annoys me, the smell of the dirty cat litter, the light bulb that burnt out, the fridge that is in dire need of a clean, or the broken door handle that makes me struggle when I need to put things away in the pantry. And heaven forbid I ever fire up the Internet without a serious purpose because 874,938 clicks and two hours later I have forgotten my name. Part of being able to focus is that you need to set your environment up so that it is conducive for focusing. You need to remove the shiny things. You have to remove anything that robs you of your ability to focus your energy!

SWIFTKICK TIP: Energy Audit

Walk through each room in your house and identify five things in each room that annoy you, drain you, or steal your focus and energy regardless of the fact you do not want them to do so. For example, something as simple as a burnt-out light bulb in the back hall can make finding something you know is in that closet more difficult, requiring more energy and time. Each time you go to the back hall in the dark, you flip on the light and are reminded that the light is not working. Yes, every time, you are annoyed and you say, "Oh crap, I need to change that," but you fail to change it. So for weeks on end, you go through the same scenario over and over. That would go on your list for the back hall because it steals your energy and time.

Schedule fifteen minutes each day in your planner to deal with your list. Change the light bulb. Tidy the pantry shelf so you can find the tuna without knocking the beans on your freshly painted toes (THAT would be a double whammy). Take a wet cloth and dust your baseboards if you see the grit every time you look at them and it bugs you. Clean out your sock drawer so you have no orphans. You get my drift. Tie up some loose ends so that you do not waste energy on this trivial stuff.

Focus is like pixie dust; it truly does allow you to fly.

Chapter 14:
WTF ARE YOU TOLERATING THAT FOR?

If you were to describe yourself, would you use the phrase "a victim of ...." Would your friends describe you as a victim? You may have a victim mindset and not even be really aware that you do. Some people seem to be a victim in almost all situations that happen in their world. They give up all their power. "Bad things" always happen TO them, and they have a "woe is me" approach to life. I call this phenomenon victimology and define it as, "the possession of an outlook, arising from real or imagined victimization that seems to glorify and indulge the state of being a victim." This mindset will not get you anywhere. It implies you have no power to change anything. And, you do. You have ALL the power, but you need to claim it.

A Bit About Victimology
People have survived tremendous ordeals and walked away insistent that they will not become victims, they will not let the situation get the better of them, and they will not let what has happened ruin their lives. Others just can't seem to see themselves as anything other than a victim, regardless of the situation. They accept NO responsibility for their own life or happiness. Victims might see problems in every

opportunity. They feel targeted, and every difficulty is exaggerated to a state of crisis.

The bottom line is that you have to educate people about how you want to be treated. That is YOUR job, not their job to figure it out. If you are in a relationship with a cheater and you keep going back, you just taught him or her that it is ok to cheat. I mean if you were not okay with you, you would leave the relationship, right? This concept can be applied across the board: relationships, professional career, money, fitness and so on.

You have to teach people what is acceptable to you. If someone is a bully in your life, you need to take a stand (safely). You need to let them know their behavior is unacceptable. Tell them you are done dealing with their crap! For example, a recently separated couple is trying to sort out the details on the phone. Each time they talk, things quickly escalate to name-calling, shouting, and belittling from one side. The other one feels intimidated and powerless. It is time to take a stand. A simple, "Look, I am more than willing to discuss all the details with you but only if we can do it with some degree of dignity, with no name-calling and no shouting. We are better than this! Call me back when you are ready to talk calmly." Hang up the phone. If the phone rings, pick it up. If the person is calm, talk. If the person loses their noodle, hang up. You have set the boundaries and if they want to engage with you, they will need to behave appropriately. **The dynamics can shift quickly: What you allow is what will continue.**

If your bully knows you are not going to tolerate something, then they move on or they change their behavior. Stand up, put the armor on, and pretend you are brave until you feel brave. Do what you need to do to give yourself the courage to face the fear.

What is the bully going to do? The obvious thing here is we know the bully is someone who is hurting. They feel their own sense of deficiency and they are projecting this on others. If you approach a bully with pity, you approach a bully with an entirely different sense of understanding and there is a significant power shift. How can you fear the pitiful? You can't pity the powerful. You take their power away. (A side note: domestic abuse is a serious situation so make sure you have the support you need and a safe place to go if, in increasing desperation and changing dynamics, your bully strikes out.)

Sometimes, you don't have to let them go, but you have to modify the relationship or change the dynamics. A victim mindset will keep you stuck. It doesn't serve your progression. Accepting responsibility for yourself and everything in your life is the quickest way to snap out of a victim mindset and access the power that has been there all along waiting to be fed and fueled!

No Base. No Build.

Stop tolerating the crap. How much can a girl take? More specifically, how much more can a girl take when she hasn't addressed the foundations for bliss and she:

- doesn't fuel her mind and body with nutritious food,
- cheats herself of quality sleep to serve others, and
- can't seem to say no in case she hurts someone else's feelings, all the while filling her plate with things that do not serve her at all?

What about you? Who is taking care of you? From now on, YOU are taking care of you. **This isn't even up for debate.**

You HAVE to commit to caring for yourself because if you are a bag of kaka, you are of no use to anyone anyway. You want to be a great mom? Take care of your needs so you feel full enough to give, to be patient, to listen, and to be flexible enough to roll with the punches.

Many clients tell me they really want to learn to be more patient with their kids or spouses and when we dig into the nitty-gritty, they are so close to homicide on any given day and so frazzled, that possessing an ounce of patience seems laughable. However, when they begin setting intentions for their day and following through, when they take charge of thirty minutes in THEIR day to recharge, they are so MUCH more patient with everyone. Patience can flourish when the foundation is there for it to do so. Taking care of YOU makes you a better person, a more caring person, and ultimately a more giving person. So streamline your life and get rid of as much of the BS as you can. You have twenty-four hours in every day and it should be full of things you love doing, not full of things that drive you bonkers and create so much stress in your life that you turn into a one-horned swamp monster!

One of my favorite mantras is: "You don't need to be a bitch, you just need to be a little bit assertive all of the time." Don't be a pushover. The first time you stand up for yourself or speak up to take care of your own interests can be terrifying. Like, poop-your-pants scary or trembling-lips scary. But holy crap, when you walk away from that situation where you just showed a little bit of muscle, you feel GOOD.

The next time you feel your guts getting tight because you can sense a situation blooming into a full on doormat-dance party, you will remember that GOOD feeling. And, even if it is with the voice of a mouse, you will speak up. (Remember that experience creates long-term change in behaviors and visualization gives you experience). You may even be surprised that people will listen to you. People will not even be that pissed off. In fact, you stating your opinions won't even be that big of a deal to most people (unlike what you had imagined in your head because of fear-based worst-case scenario assumptions) and you will walk away again, feeling STRONG. OMG, you see what's happening?

Oh yes, girlfriend, it is a sweet feeling to be able to access this sense of power that has been lurking within you for what may be years. Each time you put your foot down, just remember to do so with a genuine heart and intention to take care of yourself and you will have no reason to feel like a big meanie, even if it happens to piss someone off. That is their problem, don't make it yours!

If, on the other hand, you are just being a bitch because you can, stop it and address the real issue. You are better than that so make sure you act from a place of genuine care. Being genuine really matters, people sense it, and those that love you for you (and not because you can give them something) will support you in this desire to take care of yourself.

Tolerating You, Barely

It is not my intention to be hurtful but let's talk about how merely tolerating things or a series of things can drive you batshit crazy. Depending on who you are, whom you live with, and your life experience, you could have an enormous list of things you tolerate or a teeny tiny one. For example, two teens live in my house. One walks around with music blaring from his iPhone and the other one has a video blaring from a computer to compete with the other's music. Some days it doesn't bother me at all. Other days, it's "Turn that off, please!" Or, if you have ever had the pleasure of glancing into a teen girl's bedroom ... some days, I can tolerate it, other days I close the door and when I think it is a health hazard I ask her to tidy it up!

Ever sit beside a heavy nasal-breathing person? Or, dine with someone who very noisily chows down on ribs and it sounds like Rover has a bone? Both, given the perfect circumstances, can become the reason for a full-blown homicide for me. Seriously. Pent up tolerations can accumulate to dangerous levels. And then one day, all of the variables that create the perfect storm show up at once and you have a major issue on your hands. Funny thing is, YOU look like the crazy person because to outsiders it appears "you left your husband because he left the cap off the toothpaste" or you look like the nut job at the office because "you cracked and yelled at the person in the printing department that got something wrong." We all know it isn't the toothpaste cap or the mistake the printer made, it is the accumulation of tolerations. It is the stacking of the camel's back. Keep on piling stuff up, fail to address them when they irk you and one day, your poor, unsuspecting child walks in the room and asks an innocent question and "POW WHAM!"

When tolerations build to toxic levels, we can be propelled into action that we might not normally take. Our reactions to stacked camels may seem impulsive because we have been tolerating things beneath the surface for so long. We crack. I am sure you can imagine all sorts of scenarios where a toxic mixture of tolerations can lead to you appearing to have lost your mind. I know I can. I'll share, but you can't mock me for it!

I Am Alpha Dog

One day, the kids were at the kitchen bar scooping cereal into their mouths, slurping the milk off the spoon. (I am not a fan of that slurping sound.) The cats were climbing all over the countertop (gross). The dog was whimpering at my feet. My eyes felt swollen shut and watery. I felt off. Annoyed. (Perhaps my foundations for bliss were a bit on the shaky side?) The dog was still whimpering. The dog didn't need to go out, nor did he need anything else I could determine. He was just making this high-pitched, squeal-like repetitive noise that was driving me crazy. Then, the kids got at it, "He touched me." "She is looking at me." "IT has more room than I do!" I do not even recall specifics. It was minor ordinary "kid" stuff but I had woken up with a burr in my ass and I was already annoyed. The dog kept whimpering, the slurping of the milk, dog whimpering, the bickering, the cat on the counter, feet thumping against chairs, and did I mention the dog was whimpering?

Finally, I "snapped." I yelled from the deepest part of my gut, "I am the alpha dog!" My kids froze. I dropped to the ground.

The dog was at my feet, still whimpering. I grabbed the dog and in one swift move I got my Caesar Millan on. I threw the dog onto his back and "bit" his neck and growled from deep in my throat. I am leader of this pack! I let Rolo go momentarily and lifted my head to look at his shocked and puzzled puppy face and to spit out a mouthful of fur before I "bit" his neck and growled some more. "I am the alpha dog! Grrrrr. I am the alpha dog." (Please note the bite was more of a gummed mouthing. No dog was harmed in this apparent mental breakdown.)

When I was done asserting my dominance over the dog, I rose with another mouth full of dog hair and spit on my chin to look into the faces of my wide-eyed children. Sitting at the bar, spoons held still in front of open mouths, milk dripped into the bowls below, eyes frozen in shock. We stared at one another for a very long time, as I breathed heavily through flared nostrils. The kids dared not speak. I saw the smiles begin to creep into their eyes. I was not the entertainment this morning. Hell, no! I was the alpha dog and I had a point to make!

I started yelling. Yelling about who knows what, screaming so hard I could see myself spitting. Forcing my words out so hard they were caveman grunts, unformed and garbled. My face was red and my eyes bulged from their swollen, watery sockets. I had turned into a complete freak on the outside, yet I felt somewhat calm on the inside. I was the alpha dog. Dammit.

And at the precise moment when the kids couldn't contain their laughter any longer I realized how "that episode of stacked camel" must have looked. We all broke out into gut-splitting laughter. The shock was still apparent on their faces after seeing me spitting mad. But it didn't matter because I was alpha dog. I was done tolerating the stuff that drove me nuts and things were going to change. And even though they laughed, they kept their eyes on me because they saw that even Mommy had her breaking point and they were not certain I was completely over it yet.

SWIFTKICK TIP: How Scripts Can Save Yo' Ass and Give You Less to Tolerate

We all have a million things flung at us on a daily basis. Most of it is BS and most of it isn't even our own BS. Yet, we somehow get caught in the crossfire by nature of how it splatters. So, how do we decrease the list of things we need to tolerate?

Now that you are aware that simply tolerating things that you do not need in your life can lead you to the land of "Alpha Dog," you will begin to snub your nose at things because you are knowledgeable about the possible impact they can have on how you feel and act. Things easily snubbed are usually a little less close to us, and saying no to them doesn't create much of a ripple but some things you would like to not have to tolerate are a little harder to shake off.

Many women that I meet have a really hard time saying "no" to any request because they feel like they are being rude, feel guilty for not helping, or they do not even consider saying "no" as an option. First off, saying "no" is not always an option, but when it is, exercise your right to decide what you want to spend your time doing.

One technique that has proven itself worthy in many situations is the use of scripts. Scripts allow you to remove yourself from a situation before you walk away with a handful of extra commitments and increased stress. Scripts also do not sound like you are screaming no at the top of your lungs. Here are a couple of examples:

1. Your best friend has jumped in on the "newest and greatest candle company" trend and has decided she will start selling

candle products with a new home based business venture. She talks about **her dream** of building this business so she can spend time with **her** kids and have flexibility. She comes up with this super great (her opinion, not yours) plan about how if you hosted a few parties for her in no time she would reach Candle Company Silver Director. She shares it with you, bubbling over with enthusiasm and asks you directly for your help. Your stomach knots up almost immediately as you sense what this will mean for you. You reply with a script:

"Geez, Sarah, that is an awesome idea! I can see how excited you are about it. But I am really focusing on some personal needs and what I want right now, and I need to focus on what serves **my** intentions, so I am going to have to pass on helping you with that right now. Good luck and let me know how it goes."

Another approach I call "Beat Them To The Bail" aims to allow you to "escape" before they even get the chance to ask you for your participation.

2. You are listening to a conversation evolve and start to get the feeling you are going to be pulled into it in some manner. "Beat Them To The Bail" with a script. Opt out before they can even ask you.

    "Wow, Martha, that sounds like a fabulous project. Let me know how it works out!" or "Wow, Martha, that is a great idea! I wish I wasn't so busy or I would offer to help. Please let me know how it goes."

Slick hey? Don't even give people an opportunity to ask you if you do not want to do something. This allows you to be in control of your charity. Now that, my friends, is energy efficient. It removes you from the place of even having to say no. And, a HUGE bonus to having scripts ready to go is that it helps you keep a bunch of crap from seeping BACK into your life as you are trying to push the old crap out. This gives you a little space, a little breathing room, and a moment to THINK.

Using scripts to exit stage left can be applied across all aspects of your life. To get started, think of one area of your life where you find yourself saying yes to things you do not want to. Write out a couple of scripts using the methods above for that particular situation and memorize them. Once you have used the scripts a couple of times to reduce what you need to tolerate, you will be well on your way.

It is very empowering to feel more in control of what is happening in your life. Scripts allow you to be polite, graceful and effective. If you feel really stressed, excuse yourself from the situation with a friendly, "I will have to get back to you on that," and then collect yourself before you do! Remember, you do not need to be a bitch, just be a little assertive all of the time. Also, remember that it is okay for you to decline an invitation. Their disappointment is not your issue.

Chapter 15:
HABITS MUST SERVE YOU

All of us have habits of some kind. Our days are filled with acquired behavioral patterns that we follow (often mindlessly) until they almost become automatic.

Habits can be good and they can be bad. The mindless/automatic nature of them makes them a little dangerous when you are trying to change your life because anytime you are not "on" or aware, you have the tendency to slip back into old ways. You know, like sitting down on the couch after work and letting exhaustion take you over before you even realize what you have done. The difference between people who consistently achieve what they have set out to do and those who do not, is what type of habits they fill their days with and their level of awareness. Successful people have lives oozing with habits that serve an intention, whereas, struggling people have habits that act as an obstacle to getting where they want to go. Honestly, it is that simple.

Changing habits is another beast. I read the best quote the other day about change.

"Change is hard at first, messy in the middle, and gorgeous in the end."
-Robin Sharma

Yo, we are working our way to gorgeous but none of us can get there accidently. You have to do the work!

When I hit rock bottom and decided enough was enough in terms of my health, I immediately started restructuring my life. There are a few things you can't restructure out of a life, like tending to the needs of your children (or the fact you have them) or showing up for work. However, in those cases there could be ways to do a better job of meeting those needs while also serving your intentions. For example, you need to work out but your son needs to go to soccer. You could just drive him to soccer and spend the hour chatting with the other mothers, or you could throw on your work out gear and do your run while he is practicing soccer. You could even run laps around the soccer field or hill repeats in the park behind his field.

Back in the day, three of the habits I had that didn't serve the intention I had to regain health and wellness were:
- Coming home exhausted and collapsing on the couch watching TV mindlessly for hours thinking if I sat there long enough I would suddenly gain the energy to do something productive.
- Keeping very late hours, poor sleep habits, and because of this, I hated getting up.
- Never saying no to other demands on me.

Clearly, you can't work out if your ass is stuck to a couch or if you are too bagged to get up in the morning because you only had three hours of sleep. You may be able to use the "I don't have time" to workout excuse once, but once you restructure your life, you realize it is about making and claiming the time through priorities and mindsets.

Understanding that the old habits didn't serve my intention, I replaced them with ones that could.

- I told myself I couldn't sit down on the couch until dinner was made and served, and my workout was complete. I've morphed from a reality show junkie to not watching any TV anymore. Working out ultimately GIFTED me with more energy.
- I set the alarm to go off every night at ten o'clock to signal that it was time for bed. It served as a reminder and kept me aware. After doing that, 5:30 am wasn't so bad after all. I even grew to love the peacefulness of the morning.
- I learned a few strategies for saying no (scripts) so that I could lighten my load and take back some time in my day for myself, making it more realistic to go to bed at ten and not midnight or two o'clock.

These changes were not huge. They didn't kill me or make me feel deprived. They were a first step in refining my lifestyle to support my dreams.

Repeat after me, "Habits must serve your intentions!"

SWIFTKICK TIP: Out with the Old, In with the NEW

If you need a reminder about how to make a stopping list, jump back to the activity. You made a list of things you were going to stop doing because they were never going to take you where you needed to go. Now, we are going to examine habits and we are going to replace the habits that create obstacles with new habits that open the road to endless possibilities. Ready, set, go!

Name three habits you have right now that are not supportive of where you want to be (keep in mind, you know your own goals and intentions).

Sample: Habits that are not taking me where I want to go:
- Procrastination
- Drinking Alcohol
- Poor Sleep

Now write the list of habits down. Create a description of three new behaviors that would move you closer to your goals. It isn't as simple as "Don't procrastinate." "Don't drink." And "Don't stay up all night." Your new habits must be alternatives to what you currently do. You are not just stopping something, you are replacing it with a habit that will take you places! For example, whenever I procrastinate, I am going to set a timer for five minutes and just get started on what I am not wanting to do. Instead of drinking cocktails on a nightly basis, I will save it for special occasions and replace weekday drinks with lemon water, soda water, or green tea. Put reminders on sticky notes and place them on doors and mirrors and anywhere where you need to see them to trigger awareness so you do not slip into old patterns of behavior. Make your list and create your replacement habits and watch what happens!

Chapter 16:
IT'S ABOUT TIME

You can get more money, you can get more things, but you can never get more time. What you can do though, is gain control over how you spend your time so you can get more out of each hour you have.

Remember the days when you were in high school and the twenty-four hours in every day belonged to you and you alone? Now, as an adult woman you may find that your twenty-four hours seem like a resource that is up for grabs for anyone (husband, kids, in-laws, parents, work) to make demands on as THEY see fit. Have you ever wondered why some people are able to achieve a tremendous amount in the same twenty-four hours they have in a day and you have days where you feel blessed if you get to poop alone, have a shower, or brush your pearly whites?

I know there are times when I get all excited that I can slip away to have a bath and just veg out with a trashy magazine (okay, not really, it is usually some new personal development book). Sometimes, I secretly pour myself a drink. Only, it never goes as I plan because within minutes of sinking into the soothing water, one child comes in and feels like it is a great time to have a lengthy conversation about something while I hover under the bubbles hoping the story is quick. Shortly after, another child barges into the bathroom to discuss scheduling with me. (Because I always have my planner in the tub with me, duh?!) Before you know it even the dog is in there. Motherhood certainly throws a wrench in "me" time, however, there are some ways to carve out a little bit of it regardless of your situation.

Expanding your Day

The first thing I did when I was fat and miserable and was seeking change was I looked at my daily life and habits and thought about what I could change. (I used the same approach as we discussed in the SWIFTKICK TIP: Start With Stopping and I also replaced several habits with ones that would serve my goals.) I got a really good handle of how much time I had in a day and then I decided what my priorities needed to be to support what I wanted. I also looked at how I might need to restructure the hours in my days to make things happen. Where possible, I tried to see where I could use the same time to get more than one thing done.

When examining my time journal, I noticed that after supper I "automatically" went to the couch and once I was on that couch, I usually stayed there. Most of the time I pulled my laptop onto my lap to plan for the next day of teaching and couch-parented for an hour while I tried to watch a show and do work at the same time. I did NOTHING well. Plus, I was certainly not going to be getting up off that couch to "exercise" once I was on it. After I put the kids to bed, I was back at work until they called out for me or until I fell face first into my bed exhausted.

My days all started at six am, kids to day care, and me to work. Between five and six pm, I grabbed kids from the sitter, fed them a crappy supper, and did the best I could to get through playtime/bath time and (if

I was lucky) an uneventful bedtime for kids around eight. I would stay up till two in the morning sometimes burning the midnight oil trying to get ahead and I only got more exhausted, further behind and more disengaged. The alarm still rang at six every morning.

My two kids were small and they basically owned my waking hours. This was clear, and sometimes they owned the night as well. That is the thing about parenting: you are always on call so the best-laid plans can end up tossed aside because you have to handle the kids. If I was going to integrate exercise into my life as a single mom there were limited options.

One, it had to happen first thing in the morning and two, it had to happen at home while the kids slept, for sleep was to be my babysitter. This meant I was going to need to be up an hour earlier every day so that it was done first and out of the way. I knew there was no damn way I was going to get up early if I didn't get to sleep at a reasonable time, so I told myself I had to be in bed at ten every night. And, I told myself sleeping in was not an option. I had already decided I was going to do it; I just had to do it. There was going to be no decisions made in the morning when I didn't feel like it. Sometimes I slept in my workout clothes, other times I staggered downstairs and put my jog bra on over my PJ top and just got started. I made clothing adjustments when I got warmed up.

If sleep was to take up from ten until five and my workout was five to six, I had from six to seven-thirty to get the kids and I dressed and fed and out the door. I worked until five most nights. Five-thirty until seven-thirty was supper and kids' time to chill. Then, bedtime routine and hopefully they were in bed by eight. These were the things I was already committed to and this left TWO hours to get done what needed to get done for the next day. TWO hours. Holy hell, it was time to identify my priorities!

I had some habits to replace. I quit TV. No more "Survivor" for me. I allotted time for tasks, set timers, and I got my ass in gear! In an effort to do two things at once, I learned how to run things so that I had machines working for me so I could do other things. Dishes loaded, laundry loaded, and machines buzzing, while I worked.

I got off the couch and used the kitchen table as an office. I was more focused, I sat with better posture, I was not distracted by TV shows and I did my work in record time. By ten pm, I was exhausted but I had been productive and oddly, that was energizing. I fell asleep satisfied.

Initially, the morning workouts kicked my ass, but soon I was able to enjoy them. On weekends, I went grocery shopping with a list and I prepped my food for the week. I bought plastic lunch containers and divided it all up so I had a new version of "fast food." Chicken breasts, broccoli, big salads, tuna from the can, shrimp, breakfast muffins, and raw veggies to snack on... no one said it was glamorous. I cut out sugar as best I could. I worked out six mornings a week with NO EXCEPTIONS. (Sometimes between sets, I folded laundry that had been washed the night prior instead of doing it as a stand alone activity. I meshed what I could together.) I lost twenty pounds in twelve weeks! I focused, I planned, and I strategized. I found my sweet spot.

SWIFTKICK TIP: Lifestyle Redesign

So how do you figure out how to redesign your days to serve your purpose? How do you expand your day to fit in what needs to be done while still making sure your needs are met?

1) Return to the Stopping List and do it again, this time, you are looking for any additional time leaks. What things are you doing that are wasting your precious time? Even two twenty-minute stints on Facebook could easily be traded for a kickass workout in the backyard or basement! Ask yourself, what do you want — Facebook friends or results? Highlight all of the behaviors that

waste your time. You know you will have to make some choices. But you want this right?

2) Exchange habits. As discussed in the previous chapter, replace habits that stop you from meeting your goals with habits that will help you meet them!

3) Swap and Mesh: Where it is possible, mesh activities together so you are doing two things at once. Load the dishwasher and get laundry going. Instead of waiting mindlessly for the load to finish, do a quick vacuum then you can sit down and fold the laundry and "take a break." Get as many things moving at once! And by this I do not mean tasks that require mental focus, this is saved for the mindless stuff. For example, work out while kids have that soccer game. Run errands while your kids are at an activity or fold that load of towels while you rest between weight-lifting sets in your home-made basement gym.

4) Delegate where you can. My daughter knows that if she sits down to watch a TV show, she needs to match socks in the laundry basket. If you have kids that can help out, make a list of items that they are responsible for taking care of so you do not have to waste your time on the little things. Reward them for helping! Kids love praise!

5) Get creative! You may have to change the schedule of your day! You are in charge of when it starts and stops, so get creative. My Naturopathic Doctor told me the best quality of sleep happens before midnight so if I could go to bed by ten I would feel much more rested than if I went to bed at two even if I got the same number of hours. She was right! With a better quality of sleep, getting up at even four a.m. is not too bad. If you are a mother, you can really begin to love that quiet morning time to focus on your own needs.

One last thing to cover and my work is done! Failure. Slip-ups. Falling off the wagon. Sometimes it does happen, but what do YOU do if it does? Does this mean it is the end of the game? Does this mean you are a loser and destined to fail forever? Hell, no! It means you have a great opportunity to learn something new about what works for you and tweak your gig until you get closer to your "sweet spot!"

PART 5:
Slip, Fall, Tweak, and Rise

Looking back I can connect the dots and count my blessings. But the real art to creating the kickass OMG life you crave is getting into a frame of mind NOW that makes you appreciate every day for what it gives you, every breath for what it provides, and every moment for the lesson it bestows.

Having moved through Part One and Two you have learned a tremendous amount about how to begin creating a life you love through various strategies such as the power of perspective (mindset), getting clear, letting go, facing fear, as well as, using visualization to help align your subconscious and conscious minds so that you can move swiftly into new and wonderful places. You are excited, hopeful, and elated that you understand that success begins in the mind and that you can change your mind.

Then, you slip and fall.

WAIT. STOP RIGHT THERE. The next thing we need to address is the all or nothing mindset. Basically, for all you perfectionists out there this is for you. When people slip and fall, many give up. That's it. They failed. They are either successful or they are not. There is no in between. There is no room for mistakes. Things need to be done 100% right, or not at all! WHOA!! That is pretty harsh! Let me remind you,

"An imperfect workout done TODAY is better than a perfect workout delayed indefinitely" - Unknown

If you are unlikely to do something that you need to do to make your dreams happen because you fear you are not ready, it will not be perfect, or you may fail and that keeps you from even trying, you have an all or nothing mindset. Please release yourself from the idea that perfection exists and try to uphold an 80% on, 20% off success rate. Eighty percent is still going to take you places! Wonderful, crazy, amazingly OMG places!

We all stumble. I can tell you about that bag of Oreo cookies I inhaled last week or I can pretend that I am perfect. But pretending I am perfect doesn't help either of us now does it? (And my kids would be quick to point out my flaws.) Treat yourself like you would your best friend or child. Show yourself the same compassion you would show them. Be kind to yourself, put your slip and fall into perspective, and turn that slip-up into a learning experience that will help you do better next time! Remember, it is about finding YOUR own sweet spot and that requires tweaking. Screw ups and hard lessons give you lots of information that make tweaking very productive! You have heard it before I am sure, "it is about the journey, not the destination". These strategies you have learned can be used over and over again in any order you want to keep tweaking your life right on out of the OMG atmosphere!

Chapter 17:
OMG

We are all exactly who we are today because of the lives we have led thus far. We need to celebrate that because the lessons we can pull from our experiences are exactly what we needed to learn to manifest OMG. If life so far has been a bit of a gong show, you know things need to change and it's unlikely they are going to change on their own. Taking responsibility for what happens in your life is huge movement forward. Pairing responsibility with becoming energy efficient, using focus to fly, learning how to make sound decisions that serve you, and taking action in any combination that suits your needs and you have a powerful formula for creating YOUR OMG life.

We cannot afford to be passive bystanders of our own existence. No more focusing on what was, it is time to focus on what is and what will be.

While there are events in my life I wish I had never experienced, I have taken lessons from them and realized it is because of these experiences and these lessons that my life is OMG awesome right now. This perspective of gratitude makes me feel blessed regardless of any past heartbreak or hardship. I know in my heart that I wouldn't be here, doing what I am doing, if I had taken another path. I truly love my life as it is and I am thankful for my journey. Some of the time spent in what appeared was a "waste of time," wasn't a waste at all, but I couldn't see it then!

Pain is Real. Suffering is Optional.

Some things just happen because that is the nature of life. People die. People leave. People lie. It all hurts. Loss is real. Pain is real. You cannot do anything to stop the pain except walk through it to a place of healing. While pain is real, suffering (and how you deal with the pain) is optional. How you react to an event is your choice. How you perceive an event, is your own doing. What beliefs you attach to an event about yourself, is yours to decide.

Thinking back to Zach, the young boy that died of cancer at eighteen, and his mother's strength and grace throughout his journey is remarkable. She said many times in the video and on interviews following his death that she considered it such an honor to share the journey with Zach that she didn't have any bitterness or anger to deal with. She continually felt gratitude for having Zach in her life and was so honored to be his mother. I was left speechless by her perspective.

When my Nana passed, the pastor said that while people die, relationships do not. These simple words have had a profound impact on how I deal with loss to this day. This event changed the belief system I have about life and death. Relationships never die. I thought long and hard about this simple concept and realized how true it was. In fact, holding this mindset has brought me great joy because there have been times over the years where I have seen something that reminded me of her, or witnessed something I know she would enjoy, and I can hear her voice reacting to it.

I can hear our shared laughter. I can share these things with others who knew her and they understand. When I see things I know she would love and appreciate, my relationship with her is strengthened with her in spirit. I focus on celebrating her life, not on her death.

It also helped me deal better with my other grandmother's passing, which had happened previously and felt somewhat unresolved. I just had an ache for her. She was the hands-on, chocolate-chip-cookie baking, laughing Grandma. Her home in the country next to ponds filled with frogs and salamanders was the highlight of summer vacations as I was growing up. Knowing that our relationship was not gone helped me interact differently with my memories of her. It brought me peace. By no means am I trying to write off the loss that people feel because that is real and everyone experiences it differently. **My point is that where you focus as you move through a loss can help you to avoid drowning in it, even though you are still grieving and honoring what that specific loss means for you.**

While both grandmothers lived good lives and it was time to let them go, there are times in our lives where we need to say goodbye to people prematurely. With that comes an incredible sense of unfairness, but it still doesn't change how blessed we were to have these people in our lives for the time we did. It still doesn't take away all the shared experiences, lessons, and love shared. Changing my mindset helped me tremendously. Yes, I still felt pain and loss but by changing my focus I was able to also feel joy, love and peace.

As a mother, I am now able to use my experiences to advise my children so they can better navigate the world. If taking a few hits in my lifetime has allowed me to buffer the hits of my children, I am cool with that. I often talk with my children from a perspective of, "If I knew this at your age, here is what I may have done differently." I share my stories and experiences (within reason of course) to help them understand my humanness and my mistakes. I want them to be armed with information when it comes time to make a choice in a tough social situation and not stumble and feel clueless because they never knew they would have to make such a choice. And, most importantly I want them to OWN their choices AND their consequences. Rescuing them doesn't create stronger children; it creates a really big mess!

Creating a life I love took work. It took time alone. It took time to reflect. It took me facing fears, forging ahead, and leaping blindly. Most of that wasn't easy. No, I am not perfect, nor do I live a perfect life. In fact, at times the wheels come off and things blow up BUT I have a mindset that allows me to cope and conquer.

I am human. I am aware. I have given up on the idea of perfection. (How boring would THAT be anyway?) I have been consciously engaged in positive self-development for over a decade. I have been my own guinea pig. I have risked, failed and I have truly learned many valuable things about hope, laughter, and the mindset it takes to create an OMG life. I have forgiven myself and anyone else I needed to in order to release energy for better use. I have done my best to make amends. I have changed my language, my thinking, and my understanding of pain's purpose. Having an OMG life is not always a life without struggle. Should struggle appear, you are equipped with a mindset to step past it and move forward.

Chapter 18:
SO NOW WHAT?

Hey, you're human. Yes, you are. And humans suck sometimes. Forgive yourself, please. We are in a continuous state of blooming and we all go through these awkward times. Like adult acne, moments of unplanned vulnerability can pop up without warning, like hard conversations with your teenaged children, your boss, or your lover.

While we are in a constant state of blooming and growing we also have seasons. Winter seems to come every year regardless of our desire to spend our time relishing the summer heat and cold lemonade. Winter takes on many forms of struggle and hardship. Relationships change, tolerations become full on deal-breakers, jobs suck, people come in to and out of our lives, we experience illness and disease, we struggle with wanting things we can't seem to get, we repeat the same patterns over and over again and then complain when we keep ending up pissed off at the world and can't figure out how to get our life sorted so we can get up swinging. Sometimes we are punched hard, really hard: unemployment, unexpected failures, accidents, infertility, disease, betrayals, divorce, disability, loss and even death. And none of it is fair.

I don't believe karma really bites you on the ass, I just think sometimes life sucks.

I remember talking to someone who was expressing how overwhelmed she was with the current events in her life, "this isn't what I planned," she kept saying over and over. I tried to provide support from every angle I could and she kept saying, "This isn't what I planned." Finally, I said, "Really? Things are supposed to happen as you plan them? I don't recall ANYWHERE in my life plan that I expected to be divorced, fat, stressed out, and single parenting two kids under six. In fact, I planned my life to be very different than that. I waited until I found the man that gave me butterflies and together we dreamed about a future full of laughter and family and all the good things we are supposed to have. We loved being together so much that we considered grocery shopping fun! We married and we tried to start our family. We encountered obstacles galore and I remember watching all my friends have babies with no effort at all while I was bent over a stool in the doctor's office getting needles in my ass to try to get my body to cooperate with our desire to have children. I didn't plan that. When we finally DID have our first child, I never imagined or visualized the post-partum depression and anxiety that would follow. I never imagined how our relationship would fade or how mothering two children who were only seventeen months apart would propel me into a life of sleep deprivation and mental and emotional disconnect."

I never put that scenario on my vision board. I planned none of it but it happened anyway. I cannot explain why but I can tell you this. Every single event, moment of impact, conversation of importance, person of influence, and moment of despair has taught me something. And at every realization of a new lesson, I made the choice to take that pain, perspective, emotion, and whatever gift it gave me so I could use it to make my life better. And this is exactly what you can do, too.

CHAPTER 18: SO NOW WHAT?

We screw up. We hurt people and people hurt us. Bad things happen to good people. Sometimes it is intentional and sometimes, it is just life. Sometimes, we need to give someone up so that they can live their life to THEIR fullest potential. Sometimes, someone else has to give us up so we can live our life to our fullest potential. This is what happens as our lives unfold. Ten years ago, I couldn't make sense of what and who I had become. And I made the choice to change it. I overhauled my life, my mindset, my belief systems, and I forgave myself and anyone else who hurt me. Then, I dug deep and got intimate with "my stuff" and I pulled lessons from the darkest days of my life so that I could let go of it and move on into happiness and fulfillment.

Now, looking back, I can connect the dots and count my blessings. But the real art to creating the kickass OMG life you crave is getting into a frame of mind NOW that makes you appreciate every day for what it gives you, every breath for what it provides, and every moment for the lesson it bestows.

We don't plan the curve balls but we can learn to cope with them so that in the most stressful moments they do not totally destroy us. We can recover, AND we can flourish afterwards by having the right frame of mind. No, you might not be the same. That is OKAY. You can be different. You can be better.

It likely doesn't matter what you plan, the unplanned will still make its way into your life and sometimes the unexpected brings riches unimaginable to your closed mind. Approaching each day with the right headspace puts you way ahead of the game. All this talk about the universe delivering stuff to you because you imagine it can indeed happen but the universe doesn't just see that wish for a new job and deliver. You have to DO THE WORK. You become super clear about EXACTLY what you want. You let go of all the other stuff that isn't going to help take you to your dreams. And then, you have this amazing amount of energy available to you to NOW focus entirely on the creation of this kickass life. You get really good at focusing, streamlining, creative thought, problem solving and you understand that it is true, "Where there is a will there is a way. Period."

You reorganize your life to feed the goals. Because you are so clear about what it is you want, you begin to see opportunities that you never recognized before because back then you didn't know what you wanted or what you were hoping to find. Furthermore, because you are so clear about what you want AND you communicate that to others, people approach you to help fulfill your needs. Putting your dreams out there begins to provide the "how" because things begin to happen. Your job is to dream big and not worry about how these dreams will come to be. Have trust that the clearer your dream, the more ready you will be to recognize an opportunity that is going to help you get where you need to be.

Your job is to dream big, accept responsibility for your own happiness, and get moving.

Winter passes every year. Sometimes we have some seriously cold, dreary winters but spring always arrives. The choices you make along the way, the mindset you adopt, the friends you keep, the beliefs you feed ALL play a part in how you get through winter into another season where we will find you in full bloom.

SWIFTKICK TIP: Track Your Progress or You Miss It

Progress happens in baby steps. That is precisely why every little change you make on a given day can reap huge rewards long term. You will forget about all the baby steps and how far you have come unless you write it down. If you have been tracking things in the free downloadable journal, you will already see the power in doing this. Celebrate all progress. It matters. Each tiny little step matters.

"Every storm runs, runs outta rain. Just like every dark night turns into day, every heartache will fade away. Just like every storm runs, runs outta rain. So hold your head up and tell yourself that there's something more ... Just put your feet up to the edge, put your face in the wind, and when you fall back down keep on remembering, every storm runs, runs outta rain, just like every dark night turns into day... It's gonna run outta pain, it's gonna run outta steam, It's gonna leave you alone, It's gonna set you free."

Gary Allen "Every Storm"

Chapter 19:
GOOD LUCK, SISTER! OFF YOU GO NOW.

The moment you picked up this book and peered inside, you started a journey. If just one thing I have shared has made you more aware of your choices and actions, then you have already introduced change in to your life because of this increased awareness. If the book has given you a path to follow and a set of new approaches, it can change your life in remarkable ways like it did mine.

The SWIFTKICK TIPS and activities can continue to be done over and over as you need them. As you go through life, you will always be changing, growing, and facing new challenges so use the tools to serve your needs. Tweak your approach and find your sweet spot!

You could go back, right now, to the Reality Check activity and you may already notice how differently you perceive your life and how much more equipped you feel to face the challenges that may have seemed overwhelming to you earlier. Why? Because, now you have some tools to use to get started on making some of the changes you need to create a life you love!

It is your time and I am so excited for you! If you are standing at the bottom of a mountain and it is time to begin the climb, off you go, sister. You've got this! I might add that it doesn't have to be a dreadful climb at all. Enjoy the view, take your time, and live in the moment. You don't want to miss the wild flowers beneath your feet because you are spending all your time looking at the peak. You will get there! I have no doubt. Please, enjoy the climb.

Summary:
WTF TO OMG MINDSETS THAT MATTER

1. Sometimes, you need to jump into the abyss and have faith that things will work out even if you do not know how they will work out!
2. A baby step can be your most important step. Don't underestimate small changes.
3. WTF Moments serve as a way to make sure you are aware, accountable, and ready to get moving. They are blessings.
4. Strive for life balance but do not obsess over it.
5. Perspective makes a HUGE difference. Practice gratitude. Pay attention to the lessons.
6. Mindsets are powerful beliefs that can change your entire life. Your potential is unknown.
7. You must get off of default. Be mindful and aware.
8. You need to get very clear about what YOU want.
9. Letting go is liberating and it can move you forward very quickly. Letting go doesn't mean you never cared.
10. Creating space in your life is important. Don't be so quick to fill it up without being totally aware about what you are introducing into your life.

11. Move away from what you do not want and towards what you desire.
12. Fear can keep you stuck. You control the power you give fear.
13. Decisions determine direction.
14. Action brings you satisfaction and results.
15. You need to create a foundation for bliss. It's critical care.
16. Authenticity is your power source. Be real.
17. You need to align your conscious and subconscious minds to acquire a sense of effortlessness. Vision boards and visualization are power tools for mindset growth!
18. Focus is like magic pixie dust. It changes how you use your energy. It can help you fly!
19. You don't need to tolerate half the things you do.
20. Your habits must serve your intentions.
21. You have no control over how much time you have, but you do control how you spend it.
22. Life can be painful. How you perceive the pain determines your level of suffering.
23. Track your progress and celebrate your successes.
24. You likely will fail at some point but it is part of a successful life, if you get back up!
25. An OMG Life is possible for you. Absolutely possible. You have to do the work. Go get it!

Acknowledgements

The process of writing a book has taught me a million new lessons. It has further engrained in me that I have an endless list of things to be grateful for in my now OMG life. To begin with, I need to thank Cara Alwill Leyba for her guidance and mentorship through this entire journey. Her support has been instrumental in the successful completion of what started out as a little idea and grew into a movement.

An enormous shout out goes to my editor, Cara Lockwood, for her feedback and edits on various versions of this manuscript. Her talent to see what I was trying to say even when I didn't write it that way helped me revise my writing until I felt satisfied. When I had simply had enough and all words looked the same, Cara's feedback proved to be just what the doctor ordered. Thank you for keeping me sane. Laurie Jay, thank you for your feedback and your keen eyes when I was blinded by familiarity.

Cara Loper of Loose Lid Creative, thank you for your design skills (applied lovingly to all my requirements) to create the cover design that pops and makes me smile.

To the network of friends and social media groups that read portions of my book and provided feedback, I thank you for your candid comments and your heartfelt connections with what I shared. Your enthusiasm from my project kept me going when words were thick and heavy and the nights were long and slow. I hope that you discover in *WTF to OMG* exactly what you need to so you can create your own OMG life!

Thank you to all of the amazing women whom I have met online and whom have created wonderful educational programs and given so freely of their expertise and time. Christine Kane, your Uplevel You program pulled me from some dark days and set my life off in an entirely new direction. Erika Lyremark, you lit the fire and made me see things from an entirely different perspective during the Week Long Whip. Your book *Think Like Stripper* and your straight forward, no BS way of thinking, cleared my headspace and made room for some creative new thinking! Denise Duffield-Thomson, your book *Lucky Bitch* made sense of how I had managed to transform my own life and gave me hope that this was all just the beginning. Natalie Jill, thank you for gifting me with so many wonderful opportunities to work together and for being so supportive of my desire to better myself! And Amber McCue, your enthusiasm and offer to review my work caught me at a time when I was looking for people I admired to do just that. Thank you!

Mom, Dad and Jason, thank you for reading drafts over and over and letting me know what worked and what didn't. Your insights were appreciated and I know the initial drafts were painful to read. Really. Painful. Thank you. Terri and Larry – no words. I love you. Alex and Chiara, of all the things I want for you, happiness tops the list. Be brave. Be bold. I am always here for you.

Additional Resources

The Companion Journal for this book (PDF) can be downloaded from www.swiftkickfitness.com for FREE. Please go grab it so you can track your progress and record your journey from *WTF to OMG*!

Connect with Me!
Join in the conversation on Twitter using hashtag #wtfomgbook. My twitter handle is @SwiftKickFitnes.
Facebook.com/swiftkickfitness
Instagram @swiftkickfit
Pinterest @swiftkickfit
Subscribe to my mailing list at www.swiftkickfitness.com so that you have access to additional free resources, newsletters, special announcements and offers.

Work With Me!
Please visit my website at www.swiftkickfitness.com to learn more about products and services I have created that can support you in the creation of your OMG life, including online life coaching programs.

If you are looking for suitable resources to address some of the self-care items, please allow me to offer my suggestions:

Meal Plans & Workout Plans
- 7-Day Jump Start Program: A week worth of meal plans aimed at teaching you how to put together a meal so that it is well-balanced (complex carbs, lean protein, healthy fat).
- 4-Week Jump Start Program: Contains four weeks of meal plans, grocery lists, four weeks of workouts, recipes and further mindset work to help you set yourself up for success.

- There are additional products available at this link (more advanced workout programs & recipe books) but the ones listed above are a great place to start! The programs are extremely affordable and they are designed to teach you how to make healthy changes that are sustainable long term.

Please visit www.swiftkickfitness.com for more information about these products.

CPSIA information can be obtained at www.ICGtesting.com
Printed in the USA
LVOW06s2055211215

467401LV00018B/1433/P